LETTERS TO LOVERS

WISDOM *for*
EVERY SEASON
of YOUR
MARRIAGE

LETTERS
TO LOVERS

TOM AND JEANNIE ELLIFF

BROADMAN
&HOLMAN
PUBLISHERS

NASHVILLE, TENNESSEE

© 2003
by Thomas and Jeannie Elliff

0–8054–2669–8

Published by Broadman & Holman Publishers
Nashville, Tennessee

Dewey Decimal Classification: 306.8
Subject Heading: MARRIAGE\DATING\
SOCIAL CUSTOMS\FAMILY LIFE

1 2 3 4 5 6 7 8 9 10 08 07 06 05 04 03

Dedicated to

our children, their children, and their children's children

who are

placed in our lives

by

our loving Heavenly Father.

Our prayer is

that

they will walk in love even as

Christ has loved them.

(Eph. 5:1–2)

CONTENTS

FOREWORD

If you are looking for good, godly advice on marriage and family relationships, then you've found it! *Letters to Lovers* is a book filled with wisdom, written by a very wise couple, my friends Tom and Jeannie Elliff.

The "wisdom from above" that the Bible clearly teaches and Tom and Jeannie write about is "godly skill in everyday living." Every generation needs this skill, but *this* generation *really* needs it. Illustrated by the sage wisdom of their thirty-six years of marriage, Tom and Jeannie share practical Biblical principles that they have hammered out on the anvil of experience together.

Home building concepts of spiritual commitment, covenant, and conflict resolution are shared authentically in a way that will give you hope that you *can* build a godly marriage and family.

In these pages you'll find profound truth and penetrating realism. This is no stuffy textbook, but a heart-to-heart love letter that could only be written by a couple who have ministered to tens of thousands of marriages and families over the past three decades. Be warned! The Elliffs won't always tell you what you *want* to hear but what you *need* to hear. They know that the difficult work of building a distinctively Christian marriage is not easy. As you take on the challenge of building your home, they will exhort you to build your house upon The Rock and become a Christ follower.

There's one additional reason why you need this book: Tom's chapter to men where he lists ten questions every husband ought to ask his wife once a year is worth one thousand times the price of this book. Trust me. Read it and follow his example. Your wife, your marriage, and you may never be the same.

After reading these pages, you'll find what others have known for years, Tom and Jeannie are a heaven-class couple who have wisdom from above. May God grant you favor as you use this wisdom to build your home and family to the glory of God!

Dennis Rainey
Executive Director
FamilyLife

PREFACE

God's first institution, the family, is in trouble. Think of it this way: While each of us sat riveted to our television screens on September 11, 2001, grieving the tragic loss of thousands of lives at the hands of terrorists, another disaster of even greater proportions was unfolding. During that day (if it was like every other day that year), more than 3,571 marriages died. While we looked at the rubble of the World Trade Center and the Pentagon, on 3,571 occasions a parent said good-bye to spouse and children, never to return home again. Add to this the fact that 3,571 couples were deciding to get a divorce that day; another 3,571 were filing for divorce; 3,571 more were reaching the kind of desperation that would lead to divorce; 3,571 were starting out their married lives without the commitments or counseling that would prevent divorce.

With our attention diverted, the arch terrorist just plugged on with his timeless strategy to destroy a nation by destroying its families. In most instances we just shrugged. These were "silent deaths" noticed by the media only if a prominent figure was involved and then only in a passing tip of the hat, noting the big-buck payoff the forsaken had received. No sirens wailed; no throngs applauded the desperate attempts to save the family. In fact, those who attempted to rescue them were generally branded as meddlesome and unrealistic, right-wing, narrow-minded, Bible-thumping fundamentalists. No crowds gathered in vast arenas to mourn their passing, and no massive government efforts were mounted to prevent future incursions of the enemy into our homes. Late-night talk shows were so overburdened with interviews and commentaries on how to protect our homeland that no time was left to talk about how to save our homes. If you happened to switch to a sitcom for some relief, you would never stumble across a contemporary show portraying a traditional family in a positive light.

And the rubble? How many times have you looked at those pictures of the destroyed World Trade Center? It's like trying to take in the Grand Canyon with a box camera! Broken families leave rubble too. One-third of all live births in the United States are out of wedlock. More marriages in the future will be dissolved by divorce than death. Over 50 percent of children in public schools come from single-parent homes where they experience a much greater chance for negative life outcomes. Over 50 percent of those couples filing for marriage have first lived together out of wedlock. A major percentage of high schoolers now think that is the best way to start out. Oh, there's rubble all right, but we've just learned to live with it rather than dig out and rebuild on God's principles.

This book is our small effort to turn the tide. It is written, as you will see, from a forty-year background of ministering to members of our church family who have found themselves in virtually every imaginable situation, some incredibly happy and others tragically sad. It is written with heartfelt gratitude for our family, which has provided us with more happiness than any husband or wife, father or mother, and grandparent could expect to experience on this earth. We hope that in these pages you will sense our passion for the family. But of even greater concern is that you discover God's passion for the family, His first institution.

As for the title? Well, that will become clear to you soon enough. In case you're wondering, the "lovers" are our children and their spouses; the letters are simple expressions of the kind of counsel we have sought to give them over the years. We admit that some of that counsel was sought out, but much of it has been endured by children who obviously possess the patience of Job.

As a final word, I (Tom) must say that, in addition to the grace of God, my wife is primarily responsible for the blessings which have attended our family. Founding father and President John Adams when complimented on the joy and pride he must have had in his children (son, John Quincy Adams, in particular) said, "They had a mother!" Now we hope you enjoy reading our mail!

Tom and Jeannie Elliff

ACKNOWLEDGMENTS

From its inception, this book has been a team effort. The team, however, is much larger than you might imagine. It includes, of course, our four children and their spouses. It also must include their extended families—and ours. In addition to the counsel of God expressed through the Scripture, what we have sought to bring to the table is the accumulated counsel of several generations. We both are so grateful for our parents, grandparents, countless aunts and uncles, not to mention our own brothers and sisters. They have all been a source of blessing and encouragement to us.

Special thanks are due our wonderful and supportive church family, the First Southern Baptist Church of Del City, Oklahoma. Located as we are, right next to the nation's largest military air logistics base, we have accumulated a multitude of church friends who live around the world. They have encouraged us with their prayer support and by repeatedly asking, "When are you going to put that stuff in a book?"

Jennifer Wilson, the incredibly capable administrative assistant in my office, has worked tirelessly trying to make some sense of the pages we have handed to her. We're convinced she can read Sanskrit.

Pete Livingston, our family life minister, and his wife Debbie, have been used of the Lord to keep the family torch held high in our church with their genuine concern and love for doing family God's way.

Len Goss, chief publishing editor at Broadman & Holman, has been a friend, willing servant, and wise advisor as we have sought to get this project completed.

Dr. Robert Witty, mentor and friend, has reviewed much of what has been written. His counsel is always helpful and to the point.

We lay no claim to originality in all that we share, knowing that over the years our thoughts have been molded by countless books, seminars, and personal conversations with those who seek to see the family from a divine viewpoint.

We thank the Lord for all these friends but especially for His blessings on our family. Our desire is to be "followers of God, as dear children; and walk in love, as Christ also hath loved us, and hath given himself for us an offering and a sacrifice to God" (Eph. 5:1–2).

PART ONE

From the Parents to the Children

What Kind of Love Is This?
You Are Ready to Marry When . . .
Your Marriage: A Promise and a Picture
Heart to Heart
Making the Right Decisions
Money Matters
Your Part in the Marriage Partnership
The Ideal Father

*I*n the following pages you will meet our children and read the counsel we have sought to share with them over the years. We have four children, three daughters and a son. As of this writing, they range in age from twenty-six to thirty-four.

Our eldest daughter, Beth, is married to Tony Cox. They have eight children (five boys and three girls) ages birth through thirteen. Tony is vice president of a family-owned corporation here in Oklahoma City and a deacon in our church. He and Beth serve together as Bible teachers in our student ministry. We are privileged in that they live so close to us, just a stone's throw. That means they can come over when they want—and go home when we want. Their assignment in life is to keep us young at heart.

Our second-eldest daughter, Amy, is married to David Jarboe. They have five children (one girl and four boys) ages birth through six, and serve as missionaries in Southeast Asia. They met here in our church after David assumed the position of minister to men and missions, a position that allowed him an up-front and personal view of the country in which they now minister. Their work includes language schools, water purification projects, AIDS prevention, and a special contact with Southeast Asian orphans.

Our third-eldest daughter, Sarah, is married to Greg Mann. They have four children (two girls and two boys) ages birth through four, and live in Cedar Hill, Texas, where Greg is on staff at the Hillcrest Baptist Church. Greg and Sarah each spent a portion of their college lives overseas, Greg in Africa and Sarah in Poland. Greg's sister is our son's wife. Since their parents live in Oklahoma City, this sure simplifies our family reunions. We highly recommend it!

Our son, Jon, and his wife, Becky, welcomed their first child into their home this year. Jon pastors the Harrison Hills Baptist Church in Lanesville, Indiana. Having grown up together in our church here in Oklahoma City, we have had the privilege of walking with them through their spiritual pilgrimage. Jon and Becky are the youngest in our family. Having only recently completed seminary, they are excited about the ministry God has for them in the days ahead.

Oh yes, the letters. We composed them "after the fact" as a way of introducing the subject matter in each chapter. Yet there's nothing in either the letters or the chapters that we have not had the privilege of sharing with our children and their mates face-to-face and heart-to-heart.

CHAPTER ONE

What Kind of Love Is This?

Dear Beth,

You will never know how much we appreciated your coming to us late that night when you announced that you were "in love"! No, we were not surprised in the least by the announcement. We had been watching your developing relationship with Tony and already commented to each other that you were "falling in love." Of course, with the way you flitted around the house and incessantly brought him into our conversations, well, your news was anything but a surprise.

Beth, we are so grateful for your openness in all our discussions regarding your relationship with Tony. Your transparency, and Tony's, spoke volumes about the nature of that relationship. We would have been concerned if you had been reluctant to pour out your heart to us as you did on so many occasions.

You permitted us the privilege of pouring out our hearts to you! After all, we had prayed for you and your life's mate from the moment we first got news that your mother was expecting. We wanted you to consider prayerfully just what kind of love it was that had captured

your heart and swept you off your feet. Was this really it? Was Tony
the one who would one day propose to you? Or was God sending you
strong signals to the contrary?

   We want you to know just how much we love you, how grateful we
are to be your parents, and how excited we were to walk with you
through this special time in your life.
We love you,
Dad and Mom

Eden must have been an incredible place! God and man walked
together in perfect harmony. Adam, the first created man, was introduced to Eve, fashioned by God from Adam's own rib so that they
might share love and companionship throughout their lives. In the garden they experienced the purest and highest form of love that marriage partners have ever shared on earth. It was truly a marriage made
in heaven, a marriage which had the unrestrained blessing of God.

   But then something went tragically wrong. With a single act of dis-
obedience, Adam and Eve lost their place in the garden and fellowship
with God! That decision, made in the earliest days of human history,
affects us today. It impacts the way we love God and the way we love
one another. But we're getting ahead of ourselves. Let's go back to the
Garden of Eden and meet God's first family, Adam and Eve.

BODY

Adam and Eve's most visible attribute was the actual physical body in
which they lived. God gave them physical bodies so that they could
live in a physical world. With their senses of seeing, hearing, smelling,
tasting, and touching, they could communicate with each other and
with their environment. God commanded them to "be fruitful, and
multiply, and replenish the earth, and subdue it" (Gen. 1:28). In other
words, God placed them here to subdue, or have mastery over, the
earth and all living creatures.

SPIRIT

But Adam and Eve, those "first lovers," were more than mere physical beings. The Bible tells us they were created in the image of God (Gen. 1:27). Since God is a Spirit (John 4:24), it follows that Adam and Eve possessed a spiritual side to their personalities. With their physical bodies they communicated with their environment; they perceived information about the physical world in which they lived. And with their spirits they communed with God and received the revelation of His will for their lives.

SOUL

There was another aspect of Adam and Eve's personalities, that we often refer to as the *soul* or *heart*. This was the seat of their intellect (or reasoning), emotions, and will. It's where they thought things through, examined their feelings, and made their decisions. The soul can be compared to a photographer's darkroom. It is there that we process the information we receive from either our body or our spirit and then decide how to respond. Adam and Eve were alive—body, soul, and spirit.

WHAT HAPPENED IN THE GARDEN

God specifically communicated to Adam and Eve that, with one exception, they could eat any of the fruit in the garden. That exception was the fruit of the tree of the knowledge of good and evil. "In the day that you eat from it," said God, "you will surely die" (Gen. 2:17 NASB). Of course, you know the rest of the story. Satan came to the garden and tempted Eve, who then encouraged Adam to join her in sin. They both ate of the tree of the knowledge of good and evil—and died!

No, they didn't die in body or soul. They kept on living, having children, thinking, and making decisions. They died spiritually, cut off from intimate fellowship and communion with God.

THE BIG PICTURE

Unfortunately, all of us, as descendants of Adam and Eve, are born with sin as our nature. We do not become sinners by sinning. We sin because we are sinners by our nature. As the Bible says, "There is none righteous, no, not one" (Rom. 3:10). The wages of our sin, just like that of Adam and Eve, is death, being cut off from God and communion with him (Rom. 6:23).

GOOD NEWS

As you know, even in the Garden of Eden, God expressed His love for us all by promising that a Deliverer would come to set us free from the bondage of sin (Gen. 3:15). Then God showed Adam and Eve that our Deliverer would one day lay down His life for us, shedding His blood. As our substitute He would die in our place (Gen. 3:21). This substitute was Jesus, the Lamb of God, who takes away the sin of the world. By His death He paid the wages for our sin. Now by His resurrected life He offers forgiveness, cleansing, and eternal life to all who will trust Him. That is what is meant by the statement, "For the wages of sin is death; but the gift of God is eternal life through Jesus Christ our Lord" (Rom. 6:23).

When you trust in Christ, repenting of your sin, accepting His death on the cross as payment for your sin, acknowledging Him as your Lord, you are "born again" (John 3:1–7). By this new birth you recapture what was lost by Adam and Eve in the garden; you become a brand new creation in Christ Jesus (2 Cor. 5:17).

WHAT HAS ALL THIS GOT TO DO WITH LOVE?

The three aspects of our personality—body, soul, and spirit—are also the seat of three different kinds of love. You need to know about these three kinds of love so that you can determine just what kind of love you have for this person who has entered your life. We use the word *love* to express all kinds of emotions and attachments. We speak of "loving" God, pizza, one another, or a certain kind of dog. Obviously, in spite of using the same word, each of those "loves" is really of a different kind. When you understand the different aspects of each kind of love, you are prepared to answer the big question, What kind of love is this?

PHYSICAL LOVE

When most people think of love, they associate it with an act of physical intimacy. In fact, in our generation the term *making love* is synonymous with "having sex." The sad thing about this is that most people see physical intimacy as the first aspect of love to be enjoyed rather than a privilege to be reserved for the sanctity of marriage. The Greek word *eros* refers to this kind of love, and from it we get our words *erotic* or *eroticism*. When this idea of love is the dominant factor in a relationship, it becomes destructive. Notice what an emphasis on physical love can create in a relationship:

An improper focus on physical love creates a "demanding" relationship. How many times has moral purity been surrendered to the demand, "If you really love me, you will go all the way"? Since physical intimacy is to be reserved for marriage, those who encourage it are really acting out of a selfish motive. Under the guise of "I want to make you feel good," they are primarily concerned that their own demands be satisfied.

An improper focus on physical love encourages a relationship that is "temporal" in nature. In marriage counseling we have always been intrigued by the high rate of divorce among middle-aged people. Defining love primarily as a physical relationship is a major contributor to the breakup of these marriages. As bodies go through physical changes, people begin to wonder if they've still "got it." After all, if love and sex are synonymous, then every change that affects the human physique is seen as a threat to one's "love life."

Once a wife pointed to her husband, now in a wheelchair and paralyzed because of an accident, and said, "We can't love each other anymore because of that accident!" That experience has motivated us to ask this question of couples contemplating marriage: If either of you were severely and permanently injured before marriage, do you have a love that would still bring you to the altar even if physical intimacy was not possible? That's worth thinking about.

An improper focus on physical love leads to defrauding another and destroying trust. A fraud is one who falsely represents himself so that he can enjoy privileges that do not belong to him. A person might write a check, for instance, when there is no money in his account. To defraud, in the physical sense, would be to encourage desires that you cannot fulfill within the boundaries of Scripture.

The Bible tells us that our bodies are the temple of the Holy Spirit, then warns against defiling that temple. Yet, premarital and extramarital sex says that you are willing to lead someone into sin so that you can enjoy a few moments of pleasure. In essence you have just revealed your value system, the basis upon which you make all your decisions. You have said, "Here is the bottom line. I get what I want, in spite of what it may cost others." No wonder the major cause of problems *after* marriage is found in what took place *before* marriage. The message is this: I cannot be trusted under pressure. I get what I want, regardless.

SOUL LOVE

One kind of love mentioned in the Scripture emanates from the soul. The word describing this kind of love is *phileos.* Philadelphia, for instance, is the "city of brotherly love." This kind of love appeals to both intellect and emotion. Yet outside its proper environment, it too has inherent dangers. Look at them:

Soul love can be demanding. It depends on good reasons for a relationship to begin and continue. "Our friends say we are perfect for each other; our parents want us to get married; we have made some mistakes. Rather than confess and seek counseling, let's get married; it's too late to call off the wedding. We've sent out the announcements." This kind of love can be a trap that always leads you to look for a reason to remain in a relationship.

Soul love is often temporal. Time and circumstances have a way of changing our reasoning. How often have you been shocked to hear of the divorce of a couple wed for more than twenty years? Often you will discover that they had specific reasons for staying married. "We wanted our children to have both parents at home while growing up. Now they are gone, and so are we!"

Soul love emphasizes a person's rights. Often we have counseled individuals whose major complaint is that their partner is not granting them their "rights." "I have a right to a warm meal; I have a right to expect you to call if you are going to be late; I have a right to a clean house; I have a right to expect you to pick up your clothes. I have a right to sex when I want it." People who are consumed with their rights are ungrateful when they are accommodated and angry when they are not!

BEGINNING TO GET THE PICTURE?

Unfortunately the relationships described above are consistent with the experience of the vast majority of people who at one time thought they were in love. They were, but not in the ultimate sense made possible by a relationship with Christ. Without Him you are alive in body and soul but dead in spirit. Your love will be demanding, temporal, defrauding, and focused on personal rights. With Christ you are spiritually alive, and love takes on a whole new dimension. You can become the means through which God pours His love upon the one He has chosen for your mate.

LOVE ... GOD'S WAY

The purest love is the love with which God loves you, the love He wants to channel through you so that others might receive its benefits. That love, called *agape* in the New Testament, is precisely the opposite of the others we have examined. Notice its qualities.

Spiritual love is giving. Unlike the demanding loves of body and soul, this kind of love, God's love, seeks to give itself. "God so loved the world, that He gave" (John 3:16). The issue is not what you can receive from a relationship but what you can give to it.

Spiritual love is permanent and eternal. When Paul speaks of this kind of love in 1 Corinthians 13, he reminds us that it "never fails." When people say, "We don't love each other anymore," they are admitting they did not have the love that emanates from God. That is why all marriage counseling must properly start by determining whether the counselee has the capacity for giving God's love. This would require a true experience of salvation by faith in Jesus Christ. Seeking to solve marital difficulties without this experience is as effective as trying to take a bath without water. You can go through the motions, but nothing will be accomplished.

Instead of emphasizing one's rights, spiritual love focuses on one's responsibilities. A passage of Scripture offers incredible insight into this aspect of love. Philippians 2:5–8 instructs us to have the mind of Christ regarding one another. Paul then elaborates by reminding us that, even though Christ had a right to remain in heaven, He gave up that right and took upon Himself the responsibility for coming to earth and dying on the cross so that we might experience salvation. What a refreshing experience it would be for couples to focus on responsibilities rather than rights!

WHAT ABOUT THE OTHER LOVES?

In the following chapters you will discover that your relationship must begin with a love that honors God and flows from Him. Then He will ensure that you reach the highest pleasure and deepest intimacy in all three areas—body, soul, and spirit. The psalmist put it simply: "Delight yourself in the LORD; and He will give you the desires of your heart" (Ps. 37:4 NASB).

What kind of love is this? That is the question you should be asking as you begin your relationship. Honest answers now can eliminate great pain later on. True love begins with God and remains faithful to Him and the principles of His Word.

CHAPTER TWO

You Are Ready to Marry When . . .

Dear Tony,

We remember your surprise when we willingly agreed to give you Beth's hand in marriage. It had been obvious to us for some time that you had won her heart. You even asked how we could so readily grant our permission and give our blessing. Tony, we had been praying for Beth's husband since before she was born. Are you surprised that we would recognize him when he came along?

Tony, we especially appreciated the openness with which you and Beth invited us into those exciting days of your courtship. It was refreshing to watch the eagerness with which you both abided by the parameters upon which we mutually agreed. Both of us enjoyed the time you frequently took to visit with us, open your heart to us, and allow us to get to know you.

We also appreciated the commitments you both made to keep your relationship pure and above board. These commitments added a unique depth to your marriage relationship.

In our talk about your planned proposal to Beth, you asked us about the specific issues which needed to be settled before a couple marries. What are the signs that two people are ready to marry? We were eager to talk with you about these issues although we were certain from our previous conversations that you had already settled them in your heart.

Thanks, Tony, for wanting more than our agreement with your plans. Thanks for seeking our blessing and encouragement. We love and respect you.

Prayerfully,

Beth's Mom and Dad

A PERSONAL PILGRIMAGE

Several years ago, fresh out of seminary, our family moved to Tulsa, Oklahoma, and a new assignment. Shortly after arriving, we read a news release that shocked us. It stated that for several years in our county the courts had granted more divorces than marriage licenses. We were amazed. Little did we know then that this was true of many other counties in our state and in many other states as well. I could not have imagined that this rapidly growing nationwide trend in divorce would continue until this very day.

As a new pastor in the community, I (Tom) was determined to do all I could to stem this destructive tide. Over the next two years, I had several discussions with others who were also wondering how best to approach the issue. As we met from time to time, we noticed that we were continually being drawn to five specific issues. It seemed that, if these issues were settled by a young couple *before* marriage, their marriage was virtually indestructible. On the other hand, if any one of these issues was not settled, it seemed that the marriage was headed for severe problems often ending in divorce.

After seriously considering these issues, I noticed one common element: the Bible taught that each issue was an important element in a marriage. This knowledge caused a crisis in my own ministry. Now that I knew these five truths, would I faithfully teach them to my congregation? Since these five truths were Scripture-based, would I uphold them as prerequisites for any marriage I would perform? Integrity demanded that I remain faithful to my call, both by teaching and by applying these principles in my premarriage counseling.

It has now been twenty-eight years since I committed to following what I believe to be a Scripture-based plan in premarital counseling. I am happy to report that, of all the marriages I have performed, I am aware of only two that have ended in divorce. In both instances, one of the partners has since approached me with this confession: "In your marriage sessions, we were not totally honest in stating our willing adherence to the five prerequisites."

Of course, this is not a scientific survey, but it reveals such a radical departure from the norm that I believe it is worthy of note. In fact, I remember one man exclaiming in exasperation, "Sure, preacher, if a couple adheres to all those principles, then, of course, they will stay married!" "Right," I responded, "and that's the point!" So just what are these five Scripture-based prerequisites?

1. GENUINE SALVATION AND A DYNAMIC RELATIONSHIP WITH THE LORD

There is no more significant issue than this. It is the foundation upon which life, including a successful marriage and family, must be built. This relationship is more than some offhand acknowledgment that "We are Christians," or, "We are church members." You are only ready to marry when you both know Christ and walk with Him in a dynamic and growing relationship.

Here are four major reasons why *knowing* and *growing* in Christ is imperative when considering marriage:

First, marriage is God's plan, not man's. God designed and implemented marriage in the Garden of Eden for the purpose of fulfilling His plan for the world. Marriage is God's answer for man's desire to experience the deepest of human companionships. In fact, the more society tampers with God's marriage plan, the more readily

it embraces cohabitation or even multiple partners. Human relationships become no different than those in the animal world. Doesn't it
stand to reason that if marriage is God's master plan, those who find
most success in marriage will know the Master of the plan?

*Second, marriage is to be a covenant relationship rather than a
simple contract.* Consider the vast difference between a covenant and
a contract. A covenant builds on mutual trust, while the contract is
built on a mutual distrust that stipulates provisions for dissolution.
Marriage is a covenant between the couple being married and a Holy
God. Such a covenant is designed to be permanent and binding "for
better or worse, richer or poorer, in sickness and in health, 'til death
do us part." Just as tokens were exchanged to establish covenants in
days gone by (cloaks, belts, and swords), so in marriage today the
covenant relationship is sealed with the exchange of rings as "tokens
of the covenant." How can two people enter into a mutual covenant
with God unless they know Him?

Third, marriage pictures salvation (see Eph. 5). In the Bible
Christ is referred to as the "Bridegroom," and His church (comprised
of those who know Him) is called the "Bride." In fact, every aspect
of the marriage ceremony has a corollary in the experience of salvation. Our salvation occurs when Christ takes us as His own and
when we say, "I do" to Him. At that moment we become part of
God's family. Since marriage pictures salvation, doesn't it follow
that those being married should have experienced a previous "marriage" to God's Son? Otherwise the human ceremony is nothing
more than a hypocritical mockery.

*Fourth, as we have seen, until a person knows Christ, that indi-
vidual is dead in the spirit and has no capacity to give the kind of
pure, enduring love, which comes only from the heart of God.* How
tragic it would be for two people to enter into a marriage relationship
with the capacity to love in only a physical or soulish manner. Unless
a person is born again in the spirit, that person's love will be demanding, temporal, and defrauding, seeking selfish rights rather than fulfilling responsibilities—hardly the basis upon which to build an
enduring relationship!

2. ADHERENCE TO GOD'S PRINCIPLES REGARDING DIVORCE OR REMARRIAGE

We live in a divorce culture. Virtually everything in our society miti-gates against a marriage that will last a lifetime. Approximately 50 percent of the children in our public schools live in single-parent homes. Where will they learn that God's plan is for one woman to be married to one man for life?

Often, well-meaning but misguided couples seek to enter into a marriage when the ink is scarcely dry on their divorce papers. "We made a real mistake!" they will lament. Then with a confidence not founded on Scripture, they continue, "This time it's different. This is the real thing, and believe us, we know the difference!"

Unfortunately, statistical evidence does not support this enthusi-asm. One of the highest rates of divorce is among couples for whom such a marriage is their second, or third, or fourth.

Sometimes the church offers less than the best counsel to indi-viduals who have endured the heart-wrenching experience of divorce. Pastors are often inclined to proceed with a marriage even while har-boring doubts that God will bless the union. *I probably shouldn't do this,* they think, *but if I don't, I will lose my opportunity to minister to this couple.* In reality, to proceed without a clear conviction that God will bless the union is to forfeit any ministry he might have had.

If you have been married before, you should search the Word for God's viewpoint regarding divorce and remarriage. It is a sensi-tive issue but worthy of your diligent attention. Ask your pastor for a study guide that is balanced and scripturally sound and tell him you truly want to find the mind of God on this matter. After all, genuine love would urge upon you the necessity of seeking the kind of relationship that invites God's blessing rather than his rebuke.

Often a couple will come to the marriage altar with the belief that all it takes to make a marriage work is their own personal deter-mination. In reality, this is an evidence of pride. It suggests that they can have a successful union with or without God's blessing. Making a marriage work takes God's direct involvement. Remember, He gives grace to the humble and resists the proud.

Your marriage is a picture of what it means to enter into a covenant relationship with Christ. That is why God has stated a specific opinion about divorce (Mal. 2:16). When considering the issue of divorce and remarriage, you want to get on God's side, removing anything that would hinder His unqualified blessing.

No marriage will really succeed unless the couple comes to a point where their love of God is greater than their love for each other. Searching God's heart on the issue, and complying with His principles, is evidence that He has first place in your heart.

3. PARENTS' ENCOURAGEMENT AND BLESSING

Sadly, many parents are not invited into a relationship leading to their children's marriage. In fact, many parents do not attempt to become involved. Too often parents are surprised by the news that their children are getting married. Sometimes they find out only after the marriage has taken place. Again, some parents dismiss their responsibility with, "Well, if you think that's what you want, who are we to question your decision?" Unfortunately, many parents are failing to participate with a kind of love and concern that could bring untold joy to a young couple. Many newlyweds abandon the people God has placed in their lives to ensure their joy and happiness.

There is a vast difference between cutting the apron strings and cutting the heartstrings. Biblical precedents clearly reveal the importance of the parental blessing upon marriage and the difficulties that arise if it is absent. In spite of all a couple might assume to the contrary, they *do* bring their family relationships into their marriage.

People often argue the validity of this fact. I remember one young lady saying, "I'm getting married to get away from a domineering and demanding mother." What a hurtful surprise she suffered when, only a few weeks into marriage, her irritated husband lamented, "She's just like her mother!" A person's family, for better or worse, is a microcosmic representation of that person's world. Whatever clouds exist in the relationships with a couple's families will be the clouds that bring darkness to their marriage. The same trust and joy people experience in their home will be those they seek to bring to their own marriage.

For twenty-five years I have insisted upon a personal conference with the parents of both bride and groom prior to the wedding. You cannot imagine the shock followed by incredible appreciation when they hear that their children greatly desire parental blessing. On several occasions I have had the privilege of leading parents to the Lord as we have shared about their child's desires and God's plan for marriage.

In some instances we have agreed to postpone the scheduled wedding to wait for the bride or groom to win the heart of a questioning parent. Twice when doing this, the wisdom of waiting has been abundantly clear. On one of those occasions the couple "fell out of love," cancelled their plans, subsequently married another, and now enjoy wonderful lives with the mate God had chosen for them. On another occasion the angry and immature couple ran off, got married, and separated in less than a week. In both of these instances, one of the four parents had expressed serious questions about the advisability of marriage. It is revealing that only one of these couples abided by our agreement to wait until their parents could give their blessing.

When a bride and groom seek parental blessing and when parents grant their blessing, both are giving a gift of inestimable value. Married life without such a parental blessing is missing a key element for happiness. I remember a newlywed expressing her dilemma after about one year of marriage, "I love my parents dearly," she lamented, "and I love my husband with all my heart. I only wish my husband and my parents loved each other." She explained that the rift between her husband and her parents was bringing constant and almost intolerable sadness to her heart.

When parents are invited into the marriage process by the simple act of giving their blessing, it actually helps them to let go of their children with the comforting confidence that they are in good hands. The parents no longer feel they have to prove something to their children. After all, they have manifested the ultimate expression of confidence by entrusting their child to another. For the bride and groom, asking for their parents' blessing is an appropriate opportunity for them to express their love and appreciation for their parents. How sad it would be to come to the marriage altar knowing of a parent's disagreement. Yet how joyful it is for bride and groom to know that their parents warmly approve of their life's mate and have opened both their hearts and homes.

4. VOCATIONAL FOCUS

Here the Scripture is abundantly clear. Interestingly, this is the prerequisite for which we receive the most criticism and questions initially but the most gratitude in the end.

Ours is a society which looks to the double-income family as normative and the single-income family as abnormal. The growing rate of divorce only complicates matters. When parents insist, "You need a career in case he leaves you!" they are unwittingly setting the stage for such an eventuality. Every year secular studies are published which indicate the incredible stresses of the double-income family. The toll on that marriage, and often on the children of that marriage, is incredible and permanent. Is there a satisfactory answer? Is there an answer which does not demean the role of a husband or wife but allows each to function joyfully in partnership with the other?

The most sensible approach to this issue requires a careful examination of the biblical explanation of the roles assigned to the husband and to the wife. At the outset both the husband and wife must come to terms with the model God has established.

The Bible teaches that the groom is portrayed by Christ Himself, and the bride is portrayed by the church, those Christ has taken to be His own. With this relationship established, it follows that the Christ, and likewise the husband, is cast in the role of "provider" for the home. "My God shall supply all your need according to his riches in glory by Christ Jesus" (Phil. 4:19).

Simply put, the marriage would depart from the biblical pattern if provision for the marriage depended on the wife rather than the husband. As a practical expression of this, I have for over twenty-eight years declined to perform marriages if it was essential for the wife to work outside the home in order for them to survive financially. The husband should have a clear sense of vocational focus and be able to provide sufficiently for his wife.

Consider these often-overlooked consequences when the wife is required to work outside the home:

- Both husband and wife end up giving each other the rag ends of their lives. When they're at their best, they are apart. When they're at their worst, they are together.
- Communication suffers when both husband and wife have listened and talked with others all day and are too spent to share the same courtesy with each other. As communication suffers at home, this opens the possibility of developing communication at a deeper level with someone at work.
- The husband cannot fulfill his role as protector because he cannot impact the environment in which his wife works.
- The value of double incomes is vastly overrated when you subtract all the additional costs associated with it.
- Making the choice for both parents to work until the children come often ignores God's plan for the family. Additionally, the home's greatest financial needs will come when the wife's income is cut, often precipitating a rush to find a child care center so the new mother can get back to work. Then there is the matter of trying to adjust to a new kind of home life and a child simultaneously.
- When the wife's salary is a fallback position for family income, a husband often fails to achieve his potential. *Having* to succeed is the shortcut to success for a man.
- Children often spend their greatest amount of waking time away from home and only a few hours with parents in the evening. Of course, they become like those with whom they spend the most time.
- Since by nature ladies are often more reticent to change jobs than men, husbands tend to float from one job to the next while their wives stay at the same job, build up seniority, and often become the primary provider for the home.

Over the years I have often heard the protest, "This is not the way society is these days!" I have found that while the biblical pattern often runs counter to society, it always works! For this reason I can say that while often initially challenged at this point, I have received many expressions of gratitude from those who have put it to practice. The issue often boils down to what is most important to you, a Christ-filled home or a house with all that money can buy. Think seriously about this, because how you start your marriage has a great deal to do with how your marriage will continue.

Some years ago a young couple sat in my office in tears as I explained this principle to them. She had been sold the line that being a homemaker and mother would be a terrible waste of her intellect and education. Added to that was the fact that she had a good job with a salary sufficient to pay her husband's way through graduate school. I explained carefully the biblical pattern and committed myself to work with them if they would commit to abiding by this principle. After prayer they agreed and set out on the adventure of a lifetime.

The husband extended his time in graduate school, then found a job which would enable him to provide for their family. They both became energetically involved in their church and community. As their family grew, God gave them added grace and the ability to be proper stewards of the resources which came their way. Upon graduation his work experience coupled with his schooling caused him to be immediately given a position far beyond most men his age. As he considers the lives of fellow students who are only now struggling to begin their careers and families, he thanks God for his faithfulness to the biblical pattern.

5. A DEEPENING COMMITMENT TO GOD AND TO EACH OTHER

It was the first session in our required premarriage counseling course. If things went as desired, they would meet me at the marriage altar in approximately four months. Across from me sat a young couple eager to get done with the counseling and get on with their marriage. Even now I could tell from their exchange of furtive glances that they were having problems with some of the things I was sharing with them.

When we got to this issue, the issue of timing, the truth came out. "Look preacher," said the young man, "I don't think we need all this counseling. We know each other well and are really in love. We just want to get married. This waiting for a church wedding is her parents' idea, not ours." That statement opened the door for me to ask some probing, personal questions.

"Do you get along well with her parents, and yours?"

"Not really," was his response.

"How are things going at work?" I continued.

"Pretty tough! It's hard to be on time and everything when you're in love."

"Are the two of you sleeping together?"

"Sometimes. But hey man, we're getting married," he grinned.

"I don't recall seeing you much in church," I pressed on with my questioning.

"Well," he replied, "weekends are our only time together.

"So what about it preacher? Think you can convince her folks to let us get married earlier?"

I thought carefully about how I would respond, knowing I might never have the opportunity to visit with him again. I also knew that, under these circumstances, an improperly framed answer might just give them the excuse they wanted to run off and get married. Drawing a deep breath, I began.

I explained to this couple that God has a specific choice for each of us when it comes to marriage. His plan is for the two who marry to become one so that through that union they would accomplish more together than either could accomplish separately. For this to happen, the mate God chooses for us is the one person in all the world who will bring out God's best in our lives. God's choice for our marriage partner will be someone who makes us more holy, not less. More pure, not less. More energetic and effective, not less. More in love with Him, not less. More gracious as a family member, not less.

How do you know when it's God's time for you to get married? The answer is simple: God's time for marriage has arrived when you can give clear evidence that you and the person you intend to marry are bringing out the best in each other. If you are making a mess of each other's lives while courting, think what a problem life will be when married! God's timing is designed to bring our true character to light, to expose us for who we really are.

I asked the young couple to pray about their present relationship and what it was revealing about each of them. When they left my office, I prayed for them as well. They were at a crossroads. Several days later I returned a phone call from the young lady's mother. "My daughter wanted me to call you," she said, "and thank you for your counsel. It is obvious to her that this was not God's person for her and certainly not the right time to get married." She went on to express her gratitude to God for setting her daughter free from a relationship that was destroying her. "We feel like our daughter has finally come back home!" she said, choking back the tears. God used the issue of timing to rescue her daughter from a relationship that had brought grief to her and her parents.

ARE YOU READY TO MARRY?

When considering your readiness for marriage, look for the big yes, a yes from God, a yes from your parents, and a yes in your own heart as you honestly examine your relationship in the light of God's Word.

CHAPTER THREE

Your Marriage: A Promise and a Picture

Dear Amy,

The way you floated around when David came into your life was a source of joy and amusement for your family. We were excited about David's proposal for marriage and were confident that this was God's perfect plan for you both. Interesting, isn't it, how from our first conversation with him, we sensed the Lord might have a bigger plan than any of us imagined.

Amy, we prayed for you and for this special relationship since before you were born. We love David! He seemed to fit so naturally in our family and you in his. We admired his sense of principle and purpose from the beginning! Working side by side with him here on our staff only increased that admiration.

We looked forward to your wedding day when all eyes were focused on you and David. The two of you not only entered into a covenant relationship with God; you also were painting a picture of the beautiful relationship which exists between Jesus and all who believe in Him.

From beginning to end, this time of promise for you was a picture to all of us who witnessed your marriage.

So remember, Amy, when you and David said, "I do!" to each other, it was a reminder to all of us of the day we said, "I do!" to Jesus. The way you and David were welcomed into each other's family because of your relationship to their own child is the way we are welcomed into God's family because of our relationship with His Son, Jesus. Your marriage was more than a mere ceremony; it was an awesome time of worship and reflection.

Thank you, Amy, for loving the Lord as you do and for seeking the one man in all the world whose heart beats with yours in that love.
We love you,
Dad and Mom

We could tell the young couple sitting across from us was disappointed in the news they had just received. No, their favorite song, currently in the top ten on the pop charts would not be suitable for their wedding. It was *their song,* they explained while seeking to veil their rising anger. After all, this was *their wedding!* So why would this song be unacceptable?

Like this couple many people fail to realize the true nature of a wedding ceremony and its significance. Such people see the marriage ceremony as nothing more than an elaborate exercise designed to legalize their union, to satisfy their parents, and to impress their friends. The ceremony is something to be gotten over so they can get on with life. Yet nothing could be further from the truth about marriage.

Admittedly, some wedding ceremonies take on such epic proportions that they leave the couple exhausted, the guests weary, and the parents broke. Nevertheless, as a man and a woman anticipate their wedding ceremony, it is worthwhile for them to consider the true meaning of marriage and the picture this ceremony portrays before others.

GOD'S EXAMPLES

Throughout Scripture God uses vivid examples to convey the significance of his relationship with those who know Him. The miracle of birth is such an example. Remember Jesus' conversation with Nicodemus (John 3). Jesus said that no person could really know the kingdom of God apart from being "born again." The apostle Peter also urges us as newborn babes in Christ to "desire the sincere milk of the word" (1 Pet. 2:2).

What a beautiful picture of our role in the salvation experience! A baby is not born due to its own effort or merit. Instead, a baby is totally dependent on its parents for conception and subsequent birth. Neither does our "second birth" come as a result of our merit or works (Eph. 2:9–10). Our spiritual birth is all a work of God, "lest we should boast."

This "birth" picture is also a reminder of the eternal security of a believer in Christ. Sons and daughters did not become a part of the family by their behavior, and neither will they remain members because of their conduct. A child belongs to his father regardless! The child's behavior does have a great deal to do with the enjoyment of that privilege, just as the believer's lifestyle determines whether the Heavenly Father disciplines or blesses. Here is the truth behind our Lord's parable of the prodigal son (Luke 15).

Another picture of salvation is *adoption*. Paul urges believers to consider the fact that we "have received the Spirit of adoption" (Rom. 8:15), and as a result, we can use the intimate and endearing reference *Abba* (like our term *Daddy*) in speaking to the Heavenly Father. Think how incredibly significant this example is! In the adoption process the prospective parents think carefully about their responsibility. Though they consider the child's weaknesses and strengths, they still choose that child as their own. Adoption is a perfect description of the way God has chosen us to be his own.

GOD'S FAVORITE!

Without question God's favorite example of the relationship that exists between Himself and those who know Him is marriage. This is often typified in the marriage ceremony. Throughout the Bible God speaks of his people as his "bride" or his "wife." And the New Testament portrays Christ as the divine Bridegroom, and the church as the Bride with the relationship culminating in heaven at the great marriage supper of the Lamb (Rev. 19:9).

For many years I (Tom) enjoyed the hospitality of a home in Little Rock, Arkansas. The people in that home welcomed me with open arms and hearts. I had access to every room, all the amenities, the food, and even the vehicles if needed. These gracious people have not always felt that way about me. In fact, there was an earlier time when they would have considered me an unwelcome intruder if they had found me sitting in their living room.

What made the difference? I assure you the change had nothing to do with looks, money, or brains. However, a remarkable change occurred when, one day, I stood at the marriage altar and exchanged wedding vows with their wonderful daughter. At that moment they said in their hearts, "Welcome to the family!" Similarly, when we say, "I do!" to Jesus, the Father says, "Welcome home!" From that moment we are accepted not on the basis of our own merit but because of our new relationship with his Son. We are "accepted in the beloved" (Eph. 1:6)!

A COMPLETE PICTURE

Consider, therefore, how everything about your marriage has a divine parallel, from courtship to wedding to a fulfilling life. This deeper meaning is why marriage is more than a convenient or contractual relationship but a sacred union. Let me mention several of the ways by which God sends a strong message about the Christian life through your marriage.

PREPARATION

In the days of our Lord, courtship generally preceded the marriage. When a young man found himself smitten with a young lady, he would make specific preparations before approaching both her and her father about the possibility of marriage. First, he would carefully write out an expression of the depth of his love for her. This document (called the *ketubah*) would be read in the presence of his intended and her parents at the appropriate time, then left with her until time for the wedding when it would be read publicly. It was to be a transparent expression of the depths of his heart.

Then the young man would prepare for her the most beautiful and extravagant gift possible. He would also leave the gift with her as the deposit or earnest. The gift represented his devotion and esteem and was to be so valuable that losing it would leave him impoverished. The gift would remain with her as a beautiful reminder of his love.

Finally he would purchase a cup from which he and the father of his bride would drink as a symbol of the fact that an agreement or a covenant had been established between them. This cup would also be left in the home of his bride to be a constant reminder that when all things were in a state of readiness he would return for her.

EXPECTATION

After all these things were prepared and in hand, the young groom-to-be would arrange for a meeting in her home. There he would read his written pledge of love and present it to her. Then he would present her with the gift. (The Aramaic word *arrabon* is translated *earnest* in the New Testament.) Finally, he would partake of the cup with her father to seal the commitment. Departing, he would return to his home where he was to prepare a house for her. The time of waiting had begun.

I'm sure every young lady finding herself in this situation hoped that her husband was a carpenter! After all, he would not return for her until all things were ready. Once it was prepared, the wedding took place in a rapid and exciting swirl of activity. Gathering up his groomsmen, they would approach the bride's house with the blowing of trumpets and shouting, "The bridegroom comes!" The young man would then take the bride to his home where the marriage was first consummated. Following a period of hidden intimacy with her beloved, she was brought forth and publicly introduced at a great marriage feast.

Waiting can be such an arduous task, especially when people are in love. For this reason the groom had left the three expressions of his love with her. On those days and nights when it seemed like it would be forever before he would return, she would read the pledge of his love over and over again. She would take the earnest from its safe place and be reminded of his esteem for her. This earnest was only a token, but it spoke volumes. Then, as she walked through the house, she would see placed in a prominent place the cup, a reminder that this covenant had the authority of her father behind it. She could trust her father!

THE DIVINE BRIDEGROOM AND HIS BRIDE

Now come with Jesus from the upper room to the garden and listen with hushed reverence! It is only hours before he will take the cup of sorrows with which he finally seals us as his own, his bride. He is walking with his "intended" (represented by the disciples) and seeking to allay their fears as He goes to make preparation for us in His Father's house. Listen to His words, and you cannot help now but see a new and more beautiful significance to this often quoted passage.

"Let not your heart be troubled; you believe in God [the Father], believe also in Me. In my Father's house are many mansions; if it were not so, I would have told you. I go to prepare a place for you. And if I go and prepare a place for you, I will come again and receive you to Myself there that where I am there you may be also" (John 14:1-3 NKJV).

But what if Jesus tarried in coming for His bride (as He has!)? We can comfort ourselves with the three expressions of love which He has provided for us:

1. First, there is the Bible, filled with exciting promises of his love and imminent return.
2. Then, He has given us the Holy Spirit as the earnest of our salvation (2 Cor. 1:22; 5:5). What an incredible and treasured gift He is!
3. Finally, He has given us the Lord's table as a constant reminder that He has purchased us by His blood and will return for us! "For as often as ye eat this bread, and drink this cup, ye do shew the Lord's death till he come" (1 Cor. 11:26).

Do you now see it? Everything in the marriage relationship has a divine corollary. Marriage is a sacred union and should be lived out with the constant recognition that God is your primary audience. Your marriage is to please Him above all others, including yourself.

ONE OTHER EXAMPLE

So that the significance of this corollary will not be lost, let me give one other example of this correlation between marriage and the Christian's life. This example will help you see that where you are with God will, in many ways, be reflected by where you are with your marriage partner. Understanding this simple truth will unlock many troublesome mysteries in the marriage relationship.

Several years ago a friend asked for a few moments of personal counsel. As we visited, he opened his heart and poured out his concern for his marriage. He and his wife had reached a point beyond which they could not grow in terms of personal intimacy. In words more telling than I can repeat he explained that, for some time, his wife had been totally indifferent to his attempts for physical affection.

"It seems she always has a headache," he lamented, "or she's had a busy day, she's tired, and she has too many other things on her mind." It was obvious that their relationship was developing some serious and significant cracks.

"Just what do you think the Lord is saying to you?" I asked. He replied that he was more interested in what I was going to say to his wife! Yet I continued to press, reminding him that God sends us strong messages through our relationship with our spouse, and the marriage act itself is a picture of the filling with God's Spirit. This is symbolized for us in the Song of Solomon and specifically addressed in Ephesians 5.

I urged him to notice the comparisons between the physical act of marital intimacy and the filling of the Spirit.

1. In both instances it is the result of mutual surrender.
2. In both instances the person who violates the sanctity of the union is called an "adulterer."

3. In both instances the most telling evidence of such a union is children (born or born again) who resemble their father.
4. In both instances the primary responsibility does not take place in either the bedroom or the delivery room but in raising children to maturity.
5. In both instances maturity moves a person beyond mere feelings as an evidence of enduring love.

"As a matter of fact," I asked my friend, "just how long has it been since the Lord, your divine bridegroom, has made an overture of affection to you, only to hear that you were too tired, too busy, had other things on your mind, or didn't feel well." He hung his head and then looked up with tears moistening his eyes.

"You know, preacher, it's been a long time since I have had my quiet time with the Lord. Now that you mention it, He's heard the same excuses from me as I have been hearing from my wife!" The truth had dawned on him. God was using his wife's response to him as a perfect picture of his own response to the Lord. His real problem was not physical, emotional, or even marital. It was spiritual!

Some weeks later he told me excitedly that their marriage relationship, in every way, had never been better. Then he explained that, without mentioning our conversation to his wife, he simply went home with a determination to reconnect with the Lord in a time of daily, intimate, personal devotion. On the first day his wife had come to him as he sat reading his Bible and, putting her arms around his neck, said, "You know, when I see you taking the needs of our family before the Lord, my heart just overflows with love for you!"

There you have it! Marriage begins with a promise, an "I do!" It is a total trusting of yourself to your spouse. Your marriage is also a picture of that wonderful moment when you said, "I do!" to Jesus and were then welcomed into the Father's house, "accepted in the beloved." The Lord wants to use your marriage relationship to speak volumes about your relationship to him. Such a relationship with your spouse (and with your Lord!) is worthy of your utmost attention.

How can you know the heart of your mate? Read on!

CHAPTER FOUR

Heart to Heart

Ten Questions Every Man
Should Ask His Wife Every Year

Dear David,

We are away on our annual heart-to-heart excursion. It's hard to believe that this will be the twentieth consecutive year we have taken this personal time away to relax, refresh, and renew. As you know, it's become an important anchor in our schedule, and we really look forward to it.

When we first started taking this time away, we worried about being away from the children for that length of time. However, we discovered that God spoke to us with incredible clarity during those days. We returned refreshed with some specific goals for the days ahead and with renewed physical strength to accomplish them. Since that first trip we have eagerly anticipated our annual rendezvous with God.

Now that you and Amy are married, we want to encourage you to set aside a similar time for yourselves. Getting away together will do

*wonders for you, your marriage, and your relationship with the Lord.
Just take some time to be alone with each other and with the Lord.
Seek His heart and seek the heart of your mate. Relax; listen to Him;
listen to each other. Take time to bring the needs of your family members, your own aspirations, your struggles, before the Lord in times of
unhurried prayer.*

Well, we're off to the beach. Call us if you need us!

Love,

Dad and Mom

Every couple knows that it's possible to listen to words without actually hearing someone's heart. True intimacy in the marriage relationship requires heart-to-heart communication. Proverbs 31 teaches that
the husband of the "virtuous woman" was challenged to be a man of
integrity because "the heart of her husband safely trusts her"
(v. 11 NKJV). That is just one of the benefits of heart-to-heart
communication.

So many distractions fill our lives that couples can easily drift
miles apart, even while living under the same roof. Healthy communication is essential for a healthy marriage, but it requires the full
attention of both parties. Dennis Rainey, popular radio host and
founder of Family Life Today, once confessed that he was distracted
with a television program while his wife was trying to talk with him.
Finally, in exasperation she walked over to his chair, placed her hands
on either side of his head, turned it toward her, and pled, "Listen to
me with your face." She wanted heart-to-heart communication.

For years we have enjoyed the joyous privilege of heart-to-heart
communication. However, such communication requires honest
effort. In addition to our daily morning time together (we also each
have an individual quiet time), we have made a custom of taking an
annual getaway for our personal rest and relaxation. During this
annual renewal time we assess our relationship, refocus our priorities,
and enjoy physical refreshment and exercise. We seek to listen to our
Lord and each other—heart-to-heart.

One year the Lord impressed me (Tom) with ten questions I was to ask Jeannie. I desired to hear her heart so that as her husband I could properly respond. We found an idyllic setting at our favorite restaurant tucked away in the mountains near a beautiful lake as the perfect place for a wonderful, unhurried outdoor breakfast. The view was impressive, but I don't believe either of us was prepared for what God had in store for us!

Early that morning as we walked together from our lodge to the restaurant, I told Jeannie that I had ten questions I wanted to ask her. I encouraged her to answer each question openly and honestly and without any fear that I would become defensive. I promised that this was her time and determined to write down her answers. "Be careful how you answer," I promised, "because I will respond in love to each of your answers and with a determined effort to accommodate your desires."

Here are the questions I asked her:

I. WHAT CAN I DO TO CAUSE YOU TO FEEL MORE LOVED AND CHERISHED?

My emphasis was on *feeling* not just *knowing*. Perhaps you remember the story of the wife who endured fifty years with her noncommunicative mate. Finally she asked him, "Do you love me?" "Look," her husband replied tersely, "I told you I loved you at the marriage altar, and if things change, I'll let you know!" Of course, his answer gave her little comfort!

Verbal affirmation of affection is sadly lacking in far too many marriages, but it is a practice that pays incredible dividends. While our entire family was living at home, each of us enjoyed telling the other family members, "I love you" every day. Even now, though most of our children live some distance from us, we frequently find opportunities to communicate our love.

Causing someone to feel loved and cherished takes more than words! I was reminded of this need by Jeannie's response to my first question. We had been traveling a lot. Often we found ourselves in large groups of people with demands on one or the other of us. "I just want to know that *you* know I am along with you at those times," she confided. She wanted a visible recognition of our relationship.

Jeannie reminded me that in social settings I often became so engaged in conversation with others that I left her to fend for herself. "I know you are trying to help people," she said, "but I still want you to pull out my chair at the dinner table." Ouch! (I was beginning to wonder if I should ask the other nine questions.) Jeannie wasn't selfishly craving attention; she simply desired my acknowledgment and respect for her presence as my wife. Feeling respected by your mate has a great deal to do with feeling loved.

Growth and intimacy in marriage will take place only when each partner is doing everything necessary to ensure that the other feels genuinely loved and cherished. What others may say or do to us is always tempered by our sense of whether they truly love us. Genuine love always expresses respect.

2. HOW CAN I BEST DEMONSTRATE MY APPRECIATION FOR YOU, YOUR IDEAS, AND YOUR ROLE AS MY WIFE?

A little background will be helpful here. A few days earlier while I was preparing to lead a seminar on prayer, I read Peter's admonition for husbands to dwell with their wives, "According to knowledge, giving honour unto the wife, as unto the weaker vessel, and as being heirs together of the grace of life; that your prayers be not hindered" (1 Pet. 3:7). Moreover, I had made a mental note to remind the husbands in the audience that the effectiveness of their prayers was directly related to the manner in which they responded to the needs of their wives. Now I was attempting to follow my own (and the Lord's) counsel.

My wife is uniquely gifted as a ladies' Bible teacher. Using that gift is one of her greatest joys. Yet I had sent signals that somehow I felt her gifts were inferior to mine. Jeannie reminded me of a recent occasion when I had urged her to come with me as I fulfilled a speaking engagement. She had reminded me, "Going with you would conflict with the ladies' Bible class I teach each week." "That's all right." I had responded off-handedly, "Just get somebody to fill in for you!"

With that remark I had conveyed the impression that a responsibility she had prayerfully assumed was insignificant in comparison to what I was doing. I now realized that I was asking her to give up an assignment for which she had prepared both intellectually and spiritually just so I would not have to drive alone across town to deliver a message she had heard several times. She had assured me that she was willing to do so if I felt it was important. Yet it was obvious that I wanted her to sacrifice her important commitment merely for my own convenience.

Recently I was counseling a couple struggling with this same issue. When I asked the wife to describe what was troubling her, she said, "My husband always speaks of me as his 'better half,' but in reality I feel that my ideas, concerns, and input amount to far less than half of our relationship. I would just like to know if he really means what he says."

3. WHAT CAN I DO TO ASSURE YOU THAT I HEAR AND UNDERSTAND YOUR HEART'S DESIRES?

Jeannie's answer to this question was simple, and it brought a sense of relief to my heart. "The very thing that you are doing right now tells me that you really want to know my heart," she said. Discovering the "heart desires" of one's spouse takes time, attention, focus, and above all a determination to talk about a matter until each understands the other.

As a pastor I have had the opportunity to counsel many married couples. Over the years I have discovered that some couples have little understanding of each other. In fact, many appear to build high walls in their heart to keep their spouse from really getting to the truth. Sometimes people build walls because they would be ashamed for their spouse to discover the truth. At other times they are hiding some cherished thought which they feel their mate would not value highly.

Jeannie was encouraged that I had gone to great lengths to develop these questions, then waited for an appropriate time to ask them. I had stayed with each issue until assured I had the whole truth.

Then I had covenanted with her to respond in the affirmative to each of her answers (without argument or self-defense!). All this spoke volumes to Jeannie's heart.

4. WHAT CAN I DO TO MAKE YOU FEEL ABSOLUTELY SECURE?

I was speaking to her about security on several different levels: physical, emotional, and relational. Here again my wife's answer took me off guard. As I mentioned earlier, I had been traveling a great deal. Sometimes I left Jeannie at home alone. Since we had other family members nearby, however, I was surprised by her answer: "Install an alarm system in the house!"

This kind of protection had crossed my mind before, but I just hadn't gotten around to it. My immediate thought was to remind her that our neighborhood had experienced virtually no problems with security. I could explain just how securely our house was positioned at the end of our cul-de-sac. Or, I could give her the old "Unless the Lord keep the house" lecture.

Yet I had promised to hear my wife's heart and to respond positively, so I listened. She explained her reasons: our dog had died, the bedroom was at the far end of the house, and more. As I listened, I realized that I needed to act. In less than a week the alarm system was installed. I wanted Jeannie to see that I really meant business when I said I would respond positively to her heart's concerns.

In talking with other people, I have discovered that some individuals place emotional, moral, or marital security above the physical. Our adversary has many ways of breaking and entering our homes so that it is imperative to stand on guard and to take whatever action is necessary to bring a sense of security into our homes.

I recall one wife saying to me that, as her husband watched TV, she watched her husband. Disconcerted because of what seemed to grab his attention, she began to develop great insecurities about his moral integrity and their relationship. On many occasions I have listened to a husband or a wife voice concern over relationships which threatened the stability of their home, or perhaps a job that repeatedly placed their mate in a compromising situation. In each instance the security of the home was placed at risk.

If not addressed, feelings of insecurity or lack of confidence will hover over a home like an oppressive cloud. With their differing gifts and responsibilities, a husband or wife will often sense a threat to which the other may be totally oblivious. For a secure home both husband and wife must hear each other out on these issues, and they must respond with immediate and positive action.

5. WHAT CAN I DO TO ENSURE THAT YOU HAVE CONFIDENCE AND JOY IN OUR FUTURE DIRECTION?

I first asked these ten questions when we began to experience the "empty nest" syndrome. With our children either married or in college, the pattern of our lives began to change. I admit that we were enjoying some things about the change. What were we going to do with our newfound freedom? What were God's plans for the rest of our lives?

Now, after sharing these ten questions with groups of all ages, I have concluded that this one question should be asked often and reviewed at every stage of marriage. Notice that the question concerns *our* future direction. This question was my way of reminding Jeannie that whatever course God chose for our lives, we would obey together.

Too many couples have accepted the fantasy that marriage allows the husband and wife the privilege of living together while each does his or her own thing. Husbands in particular tend to move away from the heart of their wives by announcing their plans for the future and simply assuming that what brings joy to the husband will also bring joy to the wife.

The purpose of this important question was to say to my wife, "Whatever we do must be something endorsed by your heart as well as mine." Some men are threatened by this approach because they feel that they are surrendering authority or leadership. In reality the opposite is true. This question only encourages confidence and trust.

It shows you want to be a leader like Jesus, a servant leader who seeks the best interest of those you serve in love.

Here again, Jeannie's answer to my question surprised me by its simplicity. As a matter of fact, Jeannie and I set aside a specific time during the next few days to plan our future direction together. Our discussion excited us about the possibility of bringing to reality some things we had heretofore only dreamed of doing.

6. WHAT ATTRIBUTE OR PRACTICE WOULD YOU LIKE TO SEE ME DEVELOP OR IMPROVE?

You are acquainted, I'm sure, with people who mistakenly believe they have reached an age or a stage in life beyond which no significant decisions will ever be made. They consider that their best years, the years of greatest effectiveness, are behind them. Are we talking about older people here? Not necessarily! I've met folks in their twenties who have adopted this opinion of themselves and their possibilities.

I asked Jeannie this question because the opportunities for a more effective life are always present. Currently, one of my most admired mentors, Robert G. Witty, is enjoying amazing effectiveness at the age of ninety-six! Thousands visit his Internet Web site on a regular basis. His speaking schedule would exhaust many. He is currently working on three books. He consults with two of the world's largest mission enterprises, and to top it off, he enjoys the kind of vigorous health (like Caleb's) always associated with having a sense of purpose. His secret? An eager approach to new ideas and a readiness to change.

I learned from him that, at the age of fifty-five, he completed a Ph.D. in classical rhetoric in order to possess the credentials for founding his dream, a seminary which has trained thousands of students. "I want to be like that man!" I said to my wife, and we promptly "adopted" him. The greatest lesson he has taught me is that our utility (our usefulness to the Lord) can actually increase every day of our lives. In other words, our latest years can be our greatest years!

Jeannie had no trouble in promptly answering my question. She reminded me that while the children had been at home, I faithfully practiced a discipline which meant more to her than I imagined. We had developed the practice of rising early, having our own personal quiet time with the Lord, then meeting together for thirty minutes of unhurried conversation followed by a family breakfast. Now that the children were gone and with no push to get them to school, we still had our individual quiet times, but following that, I often scheduled early morning appointments.

"I miss our time together," she said, "and the anchor of our breakfast time each morning." Her request to resume the former practice was a sobering reminder that I was neglecting a mutually beneficial formula of togetherness for our marriage. Her request would require an adjustment to my practice of early morning appointments. I had said, "No arguments!" So once again that time together became an anchor for us as we began each day.

7. WHAT ATTRIBUTE WOULD YOU MOST LIKE TO DEVELOP IN YOURSELF, AND HOW MAY I HELP YOU IN THE BEST POSSIBLE WAY?

Each of us generally has a ready answer to this question. Jeannie, in fact, was not at a loss for an answer herself. But the vital issue centered on the second part of the question: How may I help you in the best possible way?

Being a preacher, my tendency is to think that all problems can be solved with words. If soft words don't help, use hard ones. If logic doesn't work, use the sarcastic and barbed approach. If few words don't get the job done, use many. If an appeal doesn't work, use forceful language. You get the picture!

Now it was my wife's turn to help me get the picture. She opened her heart about a part of her life in which she was seeking improvement. She told me how God was speaking to her heart. She shared that God's Spirit had long ago convicted her about a specific issue and that she was eager for change. Unfortunately, my past attempts to use "words" had only brought resentment and an eagerness to defend herself. I discovered that my past attempts to help had only made matters worse.

Her openness enabled me to discover how I could be a true partner with my wife. I began to see how I could encourage her as she sought to obey God's conviction. Simply by asking this question and by listening intently to her answer, I showed my desire to fulfill that helpful role. I was saying, "I'm on your side but as a cheerleader, not a hard driving coach!" That new approach has made all the difference in both our lives.

8. IS THERE SOME ACCOMPLISHMENT IN MY LIFE THAT WOULD BRING JOY TO YOUR HEART?

I thought Jeannie would say, "You know those big game trophies hanging in our entryway? I want more, many more of them. Come on Safari Man! I want a house full of those beauties!" I'm still stunned and a little confused as to why she didn't respond in that fashion!

Jeannie did share with me, however, that she felt strongly about my completing a writing project that I had been fussing over for some period of time. Then she shared her reason for wanting me to complete the project and her confidence that the Lord would use it. She challenged me to finish it within the year, reminding me that once it was completed I would be free in my own heart to turn my attention to other issues. Since I had promised, "No argument!" I accepted the challenge, and soon it was off to the publisher.

What most encouraged me was the fact that she also believed there was much more for us to accomplish together in the balance of our lives. She needed to hear that I also felt as she did and that I was willing to accept the challenge. If I had responded negatively, she would have wondered, *Just what will we do with the balance of our lives? Will those years be filled with uncompleted tasks and unreached goals?*

The Bible is filled with examples of men and women who proved that life is not over until it's over. Remember Caleb, Joshua's partner, one of only two men in Israel's original army who were allowed the privilege of entering the promised land? Caleb's secret of strength, the driving force accompanying him through forty years in the wilderness, was the simple fact that God had promised him a specific piece of real estate and the ability to gain it. At the age of eighty-five, he asserted his claim, "Now therefore give me this mountain!" His goal kept him going!

After years of marriage counseling, I have come to believe that few things bring distress to a wife like the failure of her husband to have clear, positive objectives for the future. Yet nothing so encourages a man as the privilege of accomplishment!

9. WHAT WOULD INDICATE TO YOU MY DESIRE TO BE MORE LIKE CHRIST?

With this question I wanted to communicate my eagerness, above all, to be like my Lord. When I perform marriages, I remind couples that there is no safer place for them in the heart of their spouse than second place as long as Christ is in first place. The best way for a man to love his wife and children is for him to love Christ above all.

Jeannie needed to see indications of my desire to be Christlike. There needed to be evidences of growth in my relationship to Him and the sense that I was actually being conformed to His image. But what are those signs? She told me that there are four visible indicators which reveal the state of my spiritual life.

Prayer, or communion with the Father, is one of those indicators. Not just occasional prayer, prayer as a matter of etiquette at mealtimes, or prayer when called upon, but a life of prayer. Jeannie told me that one of her favorite mental pictures is one where I am in the chair where I spend time with the Lord, taking the needs of our family before God.

Genuine interest in the Word of God is another sign, a hunger and thirst for the Bible and an eagerness to apply its principles. I have often said that the legacy I want to leave my children is the knowledge that God is faithful to those who live by His Word. How would a man know what it is to live by the Word if he didn't spend time in it? Jeannie reminded me that she was always encouraged when she saw that the Bible meant more to me than simply a source for sermons.

Another evidence of a heart for God is a sensitivity to sin, and promptness in putting it aside the moment God's Spirit brings conviction. Hanging on to bad habits, attitudes, friends, or practices is the first clue that a man is not practicing the lordship of Christ. A willingness to confess and repent of sin, on the other hand, is a sign of spiritual vitality.

A life marked by the fruit of the Spirit is another outward sign of Christlikeness. Fruit is the outward expression of one's inward nature. As you surrender to Christ's lordship, the Holy Spirit will produce love, joy, peace, long-suffering, gentleness, goodness, faithfulness, meekness, and temperance. This is a cluster, and where you find any one of them, you will find them all.

Your marriage partner deserves the joy of knowing that, above all else, you want to be like Jesus. Nothing will bring greater confidence than to know that Christ is running the show in your heart and in your home.

10. WHAT MUTUAL GOAL(S) WOULD YOU LIKE TO SEE US ACCOMPLISH TOGETHER?

Here is the message I wanted to send with this question: This marriage is not about me; it is about us. I believe God put us together for a reason, and I want to be sure we are accomplishing all He intended.

Jeannie and I view marriage as a life together. That was not the issue here. My concern was that we maximize the contribution we can make during our brief time on this earth. I already had some ideas regarding specific things we might accomplish together, ministries we might perform. Yet were these on her heart as well?

You cannot imagine the manner in which answering this question will open the door of partnership in marriage. You will begin to check on the progress you are making, holding each other accountable, and rejoicing together when specific objectives are reached.

We discussed goals for our own relationship, our family, and the ministry opportunities God had placed at our disposal. I discovered that, in some areas, my wife's vision far exceeded my own, while in other areas mine was a challenge to her. We were able to hammer out some clear ideas of what we wanted to see accomplished at specific periods in our lives should God allow it. We then approached life together with a new sense of excitement and purpose.

A PLEDGE

Are you willing to ask these ten questions openly, without argument, and with a mind to respond positively? Following our time together, I wrote down on a single page Jeannie's responses to the ten questions above. At the bottom of that page I wrote these words, then signed my name.

> Believing that the Lord has spoken to my heart through you; desiring to answer in the affirmative to each request; and realizing that the answer to many of them will require specific measurable action on my part, I indicate to you by this signature, my determination to fulfill these desires of your heart.
>
> Signed _____
>
> Date _____

GOING FORWARD TOGETHER

Hearing the heart of your mate is necessary for going forward together. Of equal importance is the necessity of a mutually agreed upon method for finding the will of God for your family. Is such a thing possible? That is the subject of the next chapter.

CHAPTER FIVE

Making the Right Decisions

Dear Sarah,

In our last phone conversation you asked us to pray regarding several big decisions facing you and Greg. We want to assure you that we will honor your request. Now that your family is growing, every decision takes on a much greater significance because it involves more than just the two of you.

We know that God will show you his plan and that you will eagerly follow it. That has been a character trait of yours for many years. Remember those difficult decisions the two of you made about your relationship while in college? I cannot tell you how it gratified us to see how firm and resolute each of you were in your determination to obey the Lord.

Decision-making is a key issue in every family. You seem to have mastered what it takes to make the right decisions: devotion, patience, seeking wise counsel from the Word of God along with faithfulness in prayer. Some people seem always to struggle with making decisions and then sticking by them. Many of the blessings you have in your life have come because once you clearly see the light you are determined to follow it implicitly.

We know your own children are watching you closely just as you watched us. They are learning the value of standing on God's promises. They are also witnessing a living illustration of what it means to walk by faith.

So we'll keep praying with you. Just be sure you let us know how God leads you through these crucial days.

Love,

Dad and Mom

The absence of a mutually adopted and authoritative method for decision-making spells trouble in any home. Without such a method people begin keeping score of wins and losses. You win when you get your way and lose when you don't. Decisions are made on the basis of who can talk the most convincingly, pout the longest, or shout the loudest. It's not long before a pattern develops and someone surfaces who seems always to get his or her way.

There is an even greater danger to this kind of decision-making. In the end everyone loses because each misses the critical input God desires to share through the other. The husband might know everything about automobiles, but he fails to heed the warnings of his wife who senses that the salesperson is not being truthful. She might insist that the club membership is just what they need in order to develop new friends, ignoring his concerns that it will put a serious strain on their finances.

God has a better plan—a plan so incredibly effective that, once adopted, couples begin to relish the challenge of decision-making; a plan that ensures everyone is a winner; a plan that requires no devious schemes or uncharitable attitudes. First, however, it is imperative to understand just how important it is to master the art of decision-making God's way.

Life is filled with decisions. Just think about it for a moment. Every day you must make countless decisions. While some seem relatively insignificant, others have a major impact on the course of your life and the welfare of your family. Nothing is so frustrating as an indecisive individual. Yet some people just refuse to make decisions. They drag them around like tin cans tied to the rear bumper of an automobile. Periodically a deadline comes and goes, the tin can snaps off and the decision is made by default.

Other people simply wait until they are confronted with a negative factor, like getting fired, being served with a foreclosure notice, or an overdraft at the bank. Then they make a decision, but it is always a reaction to something negative, never a positive, take-charge type of action. These people remind us of the ball in a pinball machine that goes straight ahead until it meets resistance, then reacts by moving in another direction. Their lives seem to be without a plan. They are always cast in the role of "victims of circumstances."

God specifically states that He is willing to give you clear direction for your life's path. Further, He gives specific instructions as to exactly what you must do in order to receive that direction. Look at it: "Trust in the LORD with all your heart, and lean not on your own understanding; In all your ways acknowledge Him, and He shall direct your paths" (Prov. 3:5–6 NKJV).

A CRISIS OF FAITH

Every area of a believer's life is to operate on the basis of faith. Check it out! Having been saved by faith we are also instructed to live, walk, stand, pray, fight, and gain the victory by faith. In fact, we are reminded that "without faith it is impossible to please God," (Heb. 11:6 HCSB) and that "whatsoever is not of faith is sin" (Rom. 14:23). In reality faith is not faith until it is tested. The act of making a crucial decision correctly introduces us to a crisis of faith.

Faith is, quite simply, taking God at his word and acting accordingly. Notice that faith cannot be separated from a corresponding action. It is not merely what we think or believe about God. It is acting on his revealed will. Not one person in the Hall of Faith recorded in Hebrews 11 is famous for what he or she thought or felt. All are famous for what they did in response to what God had said. Thus,

"Abel offered" (v. 4), "Enoch . . . pleased God" (v. 5), "Noah . . . prepared" (v. 7), "Abraham . . . went out" (v. 8), "Moses . . . forsook"
(vv. 24, 27), and so on.

Faith is more than trusting in some specific Bible injunction or
principle, as true as it might be. It is putting your trust in the author
of that principle, relying on Him to do as He promises. It is trusting
in the Lord with all your heart.

Faith crises will spring up in your time of dating and courtship
as well as in your marriage. You will be confronted with God's way,
which often stands in opposition to the world's way, not to mention
your own desires. How will you respond? Will you trust God with all
your heart, leaving the results to Him? We have a friend who followed God's call to the mission field even though his friends (and
family) urged him to stay home "where the girls are." Yet, in respond-
ing to that call, he was introduced to God's choice for his life's mate.
His marriage was a celebration of faith and a testimony to God's
goodness. What if he had not trusted the Lord with all his heart?

Once married, the temptation is always to set aside God's clear
path in a rush to get what and where we want. Ignoring his leading,
we begin to incur debt, strike deals, and make commitments which
severely impact our family relationships. Soon we find ourselves
locked into a lifestyle that seems more like a prison than God's prov-
idence. It should seem that way because we have not trusted in the
Lord with all our heart.

Making decisions correctly requires both husband and wife to
agree that the key element of their walk together will be trust in the
Lord. This is not some type of impulsive, blind, stepping out into
the dark. It is a prayerfully contemplated determination to walk in the
light. It means that neither will press forward without the full and
heartfelt endorsement of the other that this is God's choice for their
lives. When a couple moves forward in this fashion, they are spared
the regret and second-guessing that plague so many people when the
going gets rough. They move on, believing that God has led them and
that He will keep his promises.

AVOIDING THE BIG TEMPTATION

Energy, especially oil and gas, is big business here in our part of the United States. An up-close visit to a drilling rig reveals a crucial aspect of the operation. As the drill pipe turns, it is often twisted ever so slightly off course by the rock strata through which it travels. An instrument is positioned to check the pipe's direction. Slight, almost unnoticed deviations can, over a period of time, create such a strain that the pipe is broken. It's costly to leave over a mile of drill stem in the ground. The key, of course, is to trust the instrument, not your assessment based on the appearance of the pipe.

Pilots are confronted with a similar circumstance as they fly by instruments through clouds for long periods of time. Serious crashes have occurred when pilots have trusted their feelings, their assessment of the situation, rather than the clear indications of their instruments. The challenge, of course, is to trust the instruments.

The big temptation in decision-making is to trust your own understanding rather than the clear compass of God's Word. That is why you are exhorted to "lean not on your own understanding" (Prov. 3:5 NKJV), your own assessment of a situation, void of God's counsel.

We often are invited to pray with folks over a "surefire deal which has just fallen into their laps." After relating the incredible set of circumstances which makes it all possible and then sharing what they will do for God if it succeeds, they ask us to bless the venture. As we look into the faces of the couple, it is not unusual to find that the enthusiasm of one is tempered by the fear of the other. Often, added to this are explanations that begin with, "Now we know the Bible talks about being unequally yoked but, . . ." or, "This is going to take all we've got, but an opportunity like this comes only once in a lifetime." Red flags are flapping in the wind; warning flares are zipping through the air; God is fairly screaming his cautions, but they are consumed with their own understanding.

The idea that, in spite of God's cautions, you can make something work, especially if you promise God a little bit, is nothing more than sheer arrogance. It is more than leaning unto your own understanding; it is jumping off a cliff into your own arms. God doesn't just leave the proud to themselves; he actively resists the proud in heart. Pride says,

"I'm better at this game than God." God is determined to set that record straight!

Once a couple came to us for premarital counseling. Both were fresh from especially painful divorces and admitted that their relationship with each other had been a contributing factor. Now they considered themselves free and wanted to give God an opportunity to bless them. As lovingly as we could, we showed them how to find in the Bible God's plan for their lives. "Well," they replied, "we know that it is wrong for us to get married. If you will marry us, we will come down to the altar and get God's forgiveness. Then He will bless our marriage." (We didn't even bother to check that plan out with God!) Apparently neither did they. They separated in anger a few months after being married out of state. That's the inherent danger in leaning on your own understanding!

When the Lord cautions us to lean not unto our own understanding, He is reminding us that the big temptation is not necessarily something that is set before us. It is falling in love with our own assessment, our opinion of the situation, and ignoring the counsel of God. Making correct decisions involves the mutual determination to choose God's plan even if it contradicts our own. The key, of course, is to spend time each day in prayer and the study of the Scripture, so that your mind is conformed to His. You begin to think his thoughts and have his opinions. Your inclinations are cleansed by the word He has spoken to you (see John 15:3).

SELECTIVE DEDICATION

Have you ever noticed just how proficient we are at "selective dedication"? We choose the sins we want to avoid, the sacrifices we want to make, and the arenas in which we want to acknowledge the lordship of Christ. Yet we also choose which sins we smugly want to retain, which sacrifices we want to ignore, and which arenas of our life we want to control. To put it bluntly, that won't work!

Can you imagine the pilot of an airplane selecting which instruments he will heed and which he will ignore? He could be right on course and fly into a mountainside. Or he could be at exactly the right altitude but headed in a direction opposite his intended destination. The pilot knows that to stay on course and arrive at the intended destination he must surrender his trust to each of the necessary instruments.

Our experience in talking with married couples over the years has revealed one major cause for poor decision-making: a lack of total surrender to the lordship of Christ. No wonder the writer of Proverbs exhorts us, "In all your ways acknowledge Him," with the end result being that, then, "He shall direct your paths" (3:6 NKJV).

In our church we establish an agreement with couples who come to us for marriage counseling. We will not continue counseling beyond the initial session unless they give evidence of their surrender to the Lord by faithfulness in worship, Bible study, and stewardship. Sound harsh? Think about it for a minute. Getting God's direction for our lives, finding his mind in the decision-making process, requires that we acknowledge Him in all our ways. We are amazed at the number of people who complain that this demand is excessive. As long as they feel that God is mistaken about corporate worship, Bible study, and stewardship, they will probably not place too much stock in any of the rest of His counsel either.

For those who see the value in this approach, an incredible miracle takes place. Actually it's not so much the ministry of our counselors that assists them. Having attempted to acknowledge God in all their ways, they suddenly began to receive His clear, unmistakable, practical, and effective direction for their lives. "Thank you," they will say. "You have really helped us!" In reality the opposite is true. They have just come to the point where God Himself can help them. They are acknowledging Him in all their ways. Church attendance, Bible study, and stewardship were just initial evidences of their willingness to surrender to the lordship of Christ, the one to whom all decisions are simple!

God's prophet once spoke to his people as they begged him for counsel, "Behold, the LORD's hand is not shortened, that it cannot save; neither his ear heavy, that it cannot hear: But your iniquities have separated between you and your God, and your sins have hid his face from you, that he will not hear" (Isa. 59:1–2). This was another way of registering His refusal to lead us as long as we practice selective dedication. If you want to make decisions correctly, expediently, and effectively, then covenant with your spouse to keep short accounts with God. Confess your sin of selective dedication, surrender to the lordship of Christ, be transparent about your faults and together in your faith. "In all your ways acknowledge Him, and He shall direct your paths" (Prov. 3:6 NKJV).

CHAPTER SIX

Money Matters

Dear Greg,

Today we prayed for some couples in our church who are in serious financial difficulty. They have made decisions like so many of their friends and are maxed out on their credit cards. Now they are bouncing their bills around like a basketball. Their daily mail is filled with overdue payment notices and announcements that they have been preapproved for a number of platinum cards. Something is wrong with that picture!

As we were praying, we couldn't help but think of the financial principles you and the others in our family have sought diligently to apply. What a relief to know that you are handling your finances in a God-honoring manner and reaping the results He promises.

Greg, we remember when you first approached us for permission to propose to Sarah. You had been encouraged to finish out your college work with a student loan. We wondered after you left that night if our ground rules had seemed too strict to you: (1) You were to bring absolutely no indebtedness to the marriage altar. (2) Your wife must not be required to work outside the home in order for you to handle your financial burdens.

We wondered if, in fact, those principles might cause you to postpone your intentions. In a manner we have discovered to be characteristic, you saw them as biblical principles and a positive challenge. It took diligence (and some moonlighting), but at graduation you had no indebtedness. A few months later you took your new bride to the home you had prepared for her and continued both your ministry and your graduate education. That was a few years and four children ago, but you've never wavered from that responsibility. You have certainly fulfilled your role as provider for your family.

Thank you, Greg, for being a dynamic illustration that God's principles always work. Pray for us as we minister to so many who seem to be adrift in a sea of red ink.

Love,

Dad and Mom

Perhaps nothing so exposes our character as the way we deal with our money. Personal bankruptcies are at an all-time high in the United States. Credit card debt is crippling our national economy. Many people are so indebted at the time of their marriage that they consider a single income unthinkable. Our refusal to wait for anything we want has brought impulse buying to a scale never before imagined. Financial difficulties are applying pressure at every level of marriage and family relationships.

Sadly, the picture doesn't seem to be improving. Our consumer-oriented environment daily assaults us with the importance of the unnecessary. Most people confess that they can't afford the kind of life they would enjoy. Neither do they enjoy the kind of life they can afford.

Today as never before people are searching for answers to their financial dilemma. Is there a way out of their problems? Is there a way to experience and enjoy all God has for them? The answer to both questions is a resounding yes!

FOUR GOVERNING PRINCIPLES

We are somewhat cautious in stating that difficulties can be overcome by following some sort of specific formula. On the other hand, we have found four governing principles of finance repeatedly stated, explained, and illustrated in the Scripture. You will read about them in the paragraphs that follow. But first there is another issue to be addressed.

The Christian life operates on the basis of both grace and faith. Just as we are saved by grace through faith (Eph. 2:8–9), so we are to walk by grace through faith (Col. 2:6). Many people mistakenly believe that while grace and faith are the key elements of salvation, once we have experienced those, it is back to the old grind of keeping laws in order to merit God's blessing.

God is full of mercy, but He also operates according to principle. This means that, while His forgiveness is available through Christ, He continues to prove his mercy by giving us the grace to live according to his principles. This is important to understand. As someone has said, "God's principles are like ingredients in a package. You can mix them up according to any formula you choose. But to get what He pictures on the package you have to follow the directions." God's grace enables you to do just that.

We emphasize this because of the nature of our subject. There are a lot of rules about money out there. Many of them work, even for people who have no God consciousness or desire to enter into a relationship with Him. Yet to have the life He promises (and isn't that what you want?), you must be enabled by his grace to follow His principles.

I. GOD IS SOVEREIGN

Wrapping our intellect around the principle of God's sovereignty is difficult. Our culture places a premium on ownership and individual freedom. So much so, in fact, that it is virtually impossible for us to come to grips with the reality that we actually own nothing while God owns everything.

As a young shepherd, David brings us face-to-face with this principle: "The earth is the LORD's, and the fulness thereof; the world, and they that dwell therein. For he hath founded it" (Ps. 24:1–2). Later, as his son, Solomon, prepares to ascend to the throne of Israel, David blesses the generous offering brought for the purpose of building the temple in Jerusalem. Listen to his prayer and notice how his comprehension of God's sovereignty has matured:

> Yours, O LORD, is the greatness,
> The power and the glory,
> The victory and the majesty;
> For all that is in heaven and in earth is Yours;
> Yours is the kingdom, O LORD,
> And You are exalted as head over all.
> Both riches and honor come from You,
> And You reign over all.
> In Your hand is the power and might;
> In Your hand it is to make great
> And to give strength to all.
> "Now therefore, our God,
> We thank You
> And praise Your glorious name.
> But who am I, and who are my people,
> That we should be able to offer so willingly as this?
> For all things come from You,
> And of your own we have given You.
> For we are aliens and pilgrims before You,
> As were all our fathers;
> Our days on earth are as a shadow,
> And without hope.
>
> O LORD our God, all this abundance that we have prepared to build You a house for Your holy name is from Your hand, and is all Your own (1 Chron. 29:11–16 NKJV).

The first book of the Old Testament tells us that everything which exists is created by God. In the closing book of the Old Testament, God clearly communicates that to fail to act according to His principles is more than a simple oversight; it is actually robbing Him.

The opening book of the New Testament introduces Jesus as king or sovereign. The closing book of the New Testament reveals His sovereign power over creation, life and death, as He brings this world to an end and opens the door to eternity.

God's sovereignty means that as Creator and Sustainer He both owns and is over all things. Grasp that fact, and it will revolutionize how you handle what has been entrusted to your care. We once knew an elderly couple who owned and oversaw an apartment complex. Contrary to all the rules in such a business, they never had bad renters. Over the years the complex didn't become worn down and outdated. In fact, it seemed to grow more elegant and desirable with the passing of time. It was home to the renters who voluntarily participated in its upkeep.

Once we asked the couple their secret and were surprised at the simplicity of their formula for securing such a high-quality clientele. It seems that while one of them would show an apartment, the other would go out and carefully look at the car they drove. Depending on its cleanliness, the apartment was either affordable or totally out of reach. They felt that people would not treat a rented apartment any better than they treated their own automobile. Apparently they were on to something!

Since God owns everything and we own nothing, both his glory and our good are best served by overseeing that which is entrusted to us according to his plan. The biggest hurdle you will face is settling the issue of God's sovereignty.

2. WE ARE STEWARDS

Incredible resources are under the watch care of a ship's steward, yet he owns nothing on the vessel. He is simply the overseer of resources entrusted to his care. God's word plainly states that we are "overseers" or "stewards" of the resources our Sovereign entrusts to our care. The psalmist, while extolling the majesty of God, says of man, "You have made him to have dominion over the works of Your hands; You have put all things under his feet" (Ps. 8:6 NKJV).

As a steward your primary responsibility is to fulfill the basic requirement of any steward. "Moreover it is required in stewards, that a man be found faithful" (1 Cor. 4:2). Faithful, that is, to the desires of your master. In Jesus' parable (Matt. 25:14–30), a clear line of distinction is drawn between faithfulness and unfaithfulness. Only the faithful steward receives his master's "well done!"

In this parable we also see that faithfulness is more than just "taking care of stuff." In fact, the steward who responded in that fashion was termed an "unprofitable servant" (Matt. 25:30) and cast into outer darkness. Faithfulness as a steward means that you oversee the resources entrusted to you with your master's best interest in mind. It is the master's responsibility to provide for the steward; it is the steward's responsibility to see that the master is honored by all that is done.

Life is one great exercise of stewardship. God entrusts his resources to us, and we seek his best interest, his glory, in the way we oversee their use. E. F. (Preacher) Hallock, longtime Oklahoma pastor, was also one of our mentors in the early years of our marriage. Once, while seated in his home, the conversation turned to his battle with bone cancer and the pain associated with it. His response was not what any of us expected.

"Life is a stewardship," he said quietly, "and the last great issue entrusted to our stewardship is death. While I have been trusted over the years with significant monetary resources, including this house and our car, I have had little pain. Now God has entrusted me with pain, and I want to be a good steward, giving Him glory by the way I handle it."

As a steward you must know that a time of reckoning inevitably comes, a time to give an account for the way we have tended to our assignment. The Bible speaks of the judgment seat of Christ (2 Cor. 5:10), a time when our works will be tried "as by fire" (1 Cor. 3:15) to see if what we have done is the equivalent of gold, silver, and precious stones, or merely wood, hay, and stubble (1 Cor. 3:12–13). The issue at the judgment seat of Christ will not be whether we will live forever in heaven but how we handled what was entrusted to us here on earth. It will be a question of our stewardship.

3. THERE ARE STANDARDS

Since the great issue of our stewardship is faithfulness to the Master, it stands to reason that we would want to know his expectations, or standards, for the manner in which we are to fulfill our responsibilities. He does not leave us guessing. As a friend of mine says, "God's Word says more about how we are to behave than what we're going to get!"

Before examining God's standard in two specific areas of life, it is important to remember that, once you know them, you are accountable for living up to them. Remember God's complaint registered against an indifferent nation? "Even from the days of your fathers ye are gone away from mine ordinances, and have not kept them. Return unto me, and I will return unto you" (Mal. 3:7). Knowing may not be the equivalent of doing. Yet once we know, we are accountable for doing.

God's standards apply to both our character and our conduct. Since *being* precedes *doing*, let's first examine God's standard for our character as it relates to the issue of stewardship. Here the issue is simple: God is looking at our heart. "Riches, and honour, and life" come from a heart characterized by "humility and the fear of the LORD" (Prov. 22:4). And we are reminded that even when it comes to prayer, the "fervent prayer of a righteous man avails much" (James 5:16 NKJV).

Do you remember the caution expressed earlier in this chapter, the reminder that our walk as believers is to be "by grace . . . through faith" (Eph. 2:8)? Nowhere is this issue of greater significance than in the matter of our character, or what we are at heart. God reminds us that his ultimate concern is our "heart's condition." "These people draw near with their mouths, and honor Me with their lips, But have removed their hearts far from Me, And their fear toward me is taught by the commandment of men" (Isa. 29:13 NKJV).

It is not just doing the right thing that characterizes a good steward but doing the right thing with the proper attitude of heart. The prophet Malachi reminded Israel that God's blessing had departed because even while bringing their offerings their hearts were quietly complaining, "Oh, what a weariness!" (Mal. 1:13 NKJV). Or to put it another way, "I'm giving to the church, but I can sure think of a lot better things to do with my money!"

One of the blessings of marriage is the privilege of having an "in-house" attitude monitor. God's Word exhorts us to provoke one another "unto love and to good works" (Heb. 10:24). What better person in your life to do this than a loving, concerned husband or wife who periodically challenges you to personal revival? This is the person who, more than any other on earth, really knows you and the underlying motives behind your actions. What better person to draw you daily into a circle of prayer and devotion, seeking God's best for you and the family? A friend once said that while writing out a check for his tithe he muttered something to the effect that "this sure seems like a lot of money to give to the church!" His wife responded by saying, "If you'd like, I'll start praying that God would not bless us as much. Then our tithe will be smaller!" There's that attitude monitor at work!

God's Word also gives us the standards for our conduct regarding the stewardship of material resources. A brief look in the Book of Proverbs alone reveals clear instructions for:

- Acquiring: "He becometh poor that dealeth with a slack hand: but the hand of the diligent maketh rich" (Prov. 10:4). "Wealth gotten by vanity shall be diminished: but he that gathereth by labour shall increase" (Prov. 13:11).
- Managing: "Be diligent to know the state of your flocks, and attend to your herds; For riches are not forever" (Prov. 27:23–24a NKJV). "Without counsel purposes are disappointed: but in the multitude of counsellors they are established" (Prov. 15:22).
- Giving and tithing: "The liberal soul shall be made fat; and he that watereth shall be watered also himself" (Prov. 11:25). "Honor the LORD with thy substance, and with the firstfruits of all thine increase: So shall thy barns be filled with plenty" (Prov. 3:9–10a; see also Mal. 3:8–12).

Almost 20 percent of all the instruction given to us in the Scripture has to do with the manner in which we are stewards of the resources entrusted to us. If God is sovereign and we are stewards, then we will want to fulfill our responsibilities according to his standards. When we do, we can be assured of his supply for every need in life.

4. YOU CAN LIVE WITH GOD'S SUFFICIENCY

When you exercise your stewardship according to God's standards, He will abundantly supply your every need. It is always the master's obligation to provide for His stewards. In this case we are speaking of a Master who is the Sovereign of the universe; the One of whom Paul said, "My God shall supply all your need according to his riches in glory by Christ Jesus" (Phil. 4:19).

The issue here is never the abundance or the availability of the supply. All the resources of the universe are at His disposal. The issue is always a matter of stewardship. That's why the proper recourse is never to complain about the resources available for your use. The bottom line is that you have what He can trust you with. In the Lord's parable regarding the unjust steward (Luke 16:1–12), we are reminded that faithfulness over that which seems least is directly related to the privilege of exercising faithfulness over that which is much.

The life of the legendary George Muller (1805–1898) is instructive here. During the years of his ministry, the equivalent of approximately forty million dollars (by today's standards) was entrusted to his care as provision for his ministry with the orphans in Bristol, England. Books have been written about his faith and his life of prayer. Adding impact to Muller's influence is the incredibly detailed account he kept of ministry's needs and the manner in which God abundantly provided for each of them. Muller was such a careful steward of God's resources that upon his death virtually everything entrusted to Him had already been placed into circulation for ministry to others. Today the shadow of his influence falls across the whole of the Christian church. The supply entrusted to Muller by his Master was in direct proportion to his faith and his faithfulness as a steward.

What God did through Muller, He can do through you! There must be a point of beginning, a point when you and your family surrender in faith to the sovereignty of God, determine to live out the balance of your life as a faithful steward according to his standards, and express gratitude for his supply.

Several years ago we came home from a vacation to find our house burned to the ground. We have both commented since then about the incredible grace God gave us to walk through the days that followed. We had never felt that any of those accumulated things were really ours. They did not have a grip on our hearts. As a result we were spared the absorbing grief we have seen in others at similar times. When asked by a news reporter how we felt about losing our home, we reminded him that there is a vast difference between a house and a home.

Our house and its contents had been demolished, but our home was unchanged, or if anything, it was made stronger. We were grateful for the support of our friends and church family, the supply made available through a good insurance company and agent, the ease with which we were able to relocate and rebuild another dwelling which has provided moments of wonderful ministry and joy. In reality we see this house as another trust, another opportunity to exercise stewardship over God's resources.

Before we moved into our new house, we prayed that God would give us the grace to be faithful with it, exercising our stewardship in a manner that brings glory to Him. Now that's the bottom line, isn't it? What matters about money, or any of the other resources God entrusts to our care, is that we be found faithful.

CHAPTER SEVEN

Your Part in the Marriage Partnership

Dear Becky,

You cannot understand how blessed and happy we are that, several years ago, you said yes to Jon and are now part of our family. Having known you and your parents for so many years, it just seems so natural. In our minds you are a perfect fit for our only son, the answer to our prayers since before he was born.

Soon you and Jon will welcome a new addition to your own family. Life will change dramatically for you both as God continues to work out his grand design for your family. What an incredible joy is waiting in the wings for you!

Becky, it has been exciting for us to witness the way God's plan has been unfolding for you and Jon. You are definitely fulfilling your part in the marriage partnership. The quiet and resolute faith you have consistently expressed has been rewarded in so many ways. You are to us the picture of a godly wife, the kind of suitable companion God intends for every wife to be. Trust us when we say that we know our son pretty well and he is definitely much the better since you came into his life!

We are blessed that you are our daughter-in-law! We just wanted you to know that today we are praying that the Lord will bless you by fulfilling the greatest and most godly desires of your heart.
Love,
Dad and Mom

Making the bed is a clear picture of the value of a partnership in a marriage. Try doing it alone, and you will expend a considerable amount of time and effort just going from one side of the bed to the other. When someone else is there to help, it is a snap. (Tom draws the line when it comes to those decorative pillows, however. Jeannie knows exactly where they belong, but it's a mystery he's yet to unravel.) Of course, the roles assigned to marriage partners do require a little more time, energy, and ingenuity to properly fulfill.

SHARED ROLES

Some roles are specifically designated to either the husband or wife, and problems will occur in the exact proportion to the manner in which they are reversed. These are roles God has assigned because they are specifically suited to the unique spirit of a man or woman. Yet other roles are to be shared by both husband and wife. Generally, difficulties occur when someone is not fulfilling a God-assigned role.

"I know exactly why we have marriage problems!" an exasperated wife and mother once said. "I've heard your teaching about the roles of a husband and wife. To be frank, my husband is not fulfilling his part." After listening to her for several minutes, we asked, "But are you doing your part in the marriage partnership?" After she answered with a litany of the responsibilities she was bearing, we asked again, "But are you fulfilling your part of the partnership?" Then we proceeded to explain the importance of understanding and fulfilling what we call "shared roles."

The Bible indicates that three roles in marriage are to be shared by both husband and wife.

I. COMPANION

God made abundantly clear from the first that the husband and wife were each to be their mate's most trusted companion in life. When in Genesis 2:18, He said, "It is not good for the man to be alone" (NASB), He was not kidding. In fact the Hebrew word for *alone* sounds much like our English word *bad*. The word means literally to be divided or separated from your companion. Sure enough, that's bad!

God prepares us for marriage by creating in us the awareness that something is missing. That's just what He did with Adam, who concluded after naming all the animals that there was just no suitable companion for him (see Gen. 2:19–20).

Just what is involved in being your spouse's most trusted companion in life? Are you adequately fulfilling that role? Here are nine questions to help you determine just how well you are doing:

1. Do you know the issues of greatest concern to your marriage partner? How long has it been since you asked?
2. Do you take those issues seriously? Does your spouse see you making a genuine effort in those areas?
3. Do you really listen to your mate, listening to the heart as well as the voice?
4. Do you keep confidences? Can you be trusted to hold close those things your partner shares as something to be kept between the two of you?
5. Do you avoid hurtful humor at your mate's expense? Some spouses actually use their mates as the constant butt of their jokes.
6. Is it obvious to your mate, and to others, that you find total satisfaction in him or her? No wandering eyes? Vulgar innuendoes? Programming with sexual content?

7. Have you really allowed your marriage partner to know you? Is your spouse free to "wander the halls" in the library of your life, knowing that every door is open and no questions will be refused?

8. Do you and your marriage partner have a spiritual relationship? A relationship that supersedes the physical and is growing deeper over time?

9. Would your spouse say that you are his or her most trusted companion? Or do you have other friends with whom you share at a more intimate level than you do with your spouse?

An old man, reflecting on over sixty years of marriage, once said to us, "You know, my wife is perfect. I don't mean that she is without sin because I know she's human. But she is a perfect companion for me in every respect." We expressed a similar idea to each other once while walking together along a beach in Hawaii. We jokingly concluded that there were no people in the world either of us would rather spend time with than each other. We were amused at that thought because it sounds a little myopic. We really are each other's best friend. We think that's the way God intends for it to be.

2. COMFORTER

To *comfort* means quite literally "to strengthen or fortify." In any marriage each spouse brings certain strengths (and weaknesses!) to the marriage table. The most effective marriages are those in which partners energetically unite their strengths in fulfilling God's purpose for the family. They comfort, or fortify, each other.

When God provided Adam with his companion, Eve, she was a helpmeet for him, a suitable companion. The word *help* (Hebrew *ezer*) refers to someone who surrounds, supports, and strengthens another. Many people sing the words of the great hymn, "Here I raise mine Ebeneezer; Hither by Thy help I'm come," without having the slightest idea what it means. It is a reference to a time when Israel conquered the Philistines and subdued them by the power of God. Samuel, the prophet, erected a stone and called it "Ebenezer," or

"Hitherto has the Lord helped us," for indeed God had come to the rescue.

Your marriage partner should see you in this role, as someone whose constant desire is to build strength in the marriage union. This is especially critical if you are to fulfill the specific assignments God has given every family as stated in Genesis 1:26–28:

- To reflect the image of God (see also chapter 1).
- To rule over creation (i.e., to exercise your stewardship over God's creation entrusted to you).
- To reproduce a godly heritage (i.e., to see that others follow you, physical and spiritual children who have a heart for God).

God's plan is for a husband and wife to fulfill these assignments by mutually strengthening and encouraging each other. We once visited with a married couple who had just survived a trying period in which both had experienced some serious physical difficulties. Their cheerful countenance and positive nature seemed so out of character with their circumstances. "We're just like those two circus clowns doing somersaults," the wife said. "When one gets down, the other one pulls him up!" That is a great picture of genuine comfort and encouragement! Two people were working together, sharing their strengths to overcome their weaknesses.

3. COMPLETION

How many times have you heard a man refer to his wife as his "better half"? In most cases he is right! But another truth is hidden in that statement: From the beginning God wanted a husband and wife to understand that the two of them formed one special union and neither would be complete without the other. The manner in which Eve was created from Adam's rib indicated that each was the completion of the other. The two of them were "one flesh" (Gen. 2:24).

The significance of two people becoming "one flesh" before God is profound. This means that your spouse is more than simply useful; he or she is absolutely essential. God has brought you together because only by being together can you fulfill all his great plan for your lives.

United, focused strength has incredible power. The collected rays of sunlight can be focused in such a fashion that it creates heat intense enough to start a fire. The impact of a hammer focused on the small point of a nail can cause it to penetrate a thick board. The focused firepower of a military detachment can create a breach in the strongest of fortifications. Similarly, the collected and focused strengths of a husband and wife can be used to complete successfully every assignment God gives them.

Unfortunately, many couples do not work together. In fact, some partners are more successful at tearing down their mates than they are at contributing to their strength. They are under the false assumption that one is better than two. They ignore the strengths, counsel, insight, and discernment the other can contribute, and thus their marriage begins to self-destruct.

Many marriage partners communicate the idea that their spouse is enjoyable but not valuable. Value is communicated by whom you focus on and are faithful to. Marriage partners often send strong signals that their spouse is simply not valuable by their lack of attentiveness and by unfaithfulness (whether mental, visual, or emotional). They leave their partners with the impression that it's nice having them around but not absolutely necessary. It is imperative that you see your marriage partner as God's gift to you, a gift without which you would be incomplete in every way.

THROUGH LIFE TOGETHER

Recently, at the funeral of a friend's wife, the pastor looked out across the congregation and said, "This memorial is as much about the husband who sits here as about his wife whose earthly body lies in the casket." He then related how her husband had loved and provided for her every need during their fifty-eight years of marriage. The last thirty-eight years had been especially difficult, complicated by his wife's debilitating illness which, in the end, was the cause of her death. For much of that time he was unable to leave her side because of the emotional distress it caused her.

The pastor told how the woman's husband had graciously side-stepped a compliment given him for his faithfulness. "We married each other for better or for worse and pledged to be faithful unto death," he said. "I only did what I said I would do and what she would have done for me. Yes, there were difficult moments, but we were a good team, and I was proud and blessed to be her husband. I will greatly miss her!"

There's the picture—companion, comforter, completion!

CHAPTER EIGHT

The Ideal Father

Dear Jon,

Now that you are a father, I wanted to let you know just how proud I am of you. You're doing a great job! I just wish I had approached fatherhood with the diligence and devotion you are displaying. At our last family reunion, Jeannie and I looked at our growing family (twenty-seven and counting!) and just marveled at the grace of God.

I am especially encouraged by the fact that you take seriously your role as a father. After all, a father is a child's first picture of God, so you surely don't want to slip up in that key area of responsibility. It's not an easy job, is it? But I know you are drawing on the promise of God's sufficient grace, strength, and wisdom.

Recently I've been thinking through what I believe are some key attributes every father should possess. Since our model is God, our Heavenly Father, there are sure plenty of places to turn in the Scriptures for help. You'll see that I have used the Lord's parable of the prodigal son (Luke 15:11–32) as a point of reference for my thinking.

I am honored by you, my son. You are an incredible example of fatherhood as God intended it. Your own efforts in this critical arena both humble and challenge me. Both time and eternity will reveal the value of the attention you are giving to doing it right. You are indeed building a legacy of faith and faithfulness.

Blessings on you, man of God!

Love,

Dad

Recently I ran across some definitions of a father that any man blessed with that privilege will appreciate.

- A father is one who endures the agony of childbirth . . . without an anesthetic.
- A father is the ultimate example of faith. He is willing to let his daughter marry a creep so she might produce grand-children who are absolutely beautiful.
- A father is one who never mastered the English language. He's yet to figure out how it is that *maybe* means *sure,* or "I'll think about it" means "I'll pay for it."
- A father must learn the art of convoluted reasoning: "I would have gotten you a better Father's Day gift, but you didn't give me enough money!"
- A father must constantly keep things in perspective, maintaining his cool even though he's certain his six-year-old's T-ball coach is destroying his future chances for the Olympics.
- A father must learn to scowl when looking at a child's report card—even when it reveals better grades than he ever received in his life.

THE PROPER DEFINITION

Fatherhood is serious business. It requires the best of a man's diligence and devotion. After all, a father is a child's first picture of God!

Nowhere is that truth more evident than when attempting to convince someone to approach the Heavenly Father with absolute trust. It's difficult to grasp the security of your salvation, for instance, if your own earthly father called it quits on his marriage and family responsibilities.

The story of the Prodigal Son (Luke 15:11–32) is one of the Lord's most often-referenced parables. While on the surface it appears to be a tale of two sons, it is really a story about one father and his love for his family. Of course, the father in our Lord's parable is a picture of our Heavenly Father and his perfect love for his children. From the parable, I (Tom) have gleaned what I call the "Ten Commandments for the Ideal Father."

1. Do not allow past disappointments to alter your present determination.

"Dad, I'm unwilling to wait for what I want," said the father's youngest son. "I want my part of the family estate. And I want it now!" Having divided out his estate to his sons, the father must have watched with a broken heart as his youngest son "gathered all together, and took his journey into a far country, and there wasted his substance with riotous living" (Luke 15:13).

It had to hurt when word of his son's disappointing behavior began to drift back home. Everything he had been taught was cast aside. Godless companions, foolish spending, and sexual promiscuity left him with neither inner nor outer resources with which to face the inevitable famine. His ship was on the rocks. The father's disappointment must have alternately expressed itself as grief, then anger. His son's behavior was humiliating, to say the least. He must have been tempted to ask, "Where did I go wrong? What crucial training did I overlook?"

Without question, earthly fathers share to some degree in their children's failures. And to whatever degree that is the case, you should confess, repent, and seek to recover what was lost. But it is a myth to think that perfect fathering will produce perfect children. The Edenic experience of the Heavenly Father's first two "kids" is evidence enough. He is a perfect Father, but his children have been a frequent disappointment to him!

Frequently fathers speak as if they have simply given up. Sometimes they give the impression that they have anxiously awaited the child's arrival at a certain age or stage in life beyond which they no longer feel a sense of personal responsibility. Recently I heard a father exclaim with a sigh and a grin, "Well, you know how it is, preacher. After they reach this age, you can't do much except keep food on the table and shoes on their feet." He had effectively retired from fathering his twelve-year-old.

One day my son startled me with an "out of the blue" statement. "You know, Dad, one of the greatest gifts you ever gave me was the confidence that you would never give up on me. That has really blessed my life." As we talked, I discovered that he could remember several occasions when I had said, "Son, that is not proper behavior. You are a better man than that. You may think that one day I will just give up and you will win, but it will never happen. I will never stop believing, praying, and working with you so that you will be the man God wants you to be." Somehow my son had found extraordinary comfort and encouragement in those words.

Notice the father in our Lord's parable. Disappointed yes. Defeated no! He had obviously pondered over, prayed through, and planned for his son's return. Even after an extended time of separation, he is seen looking down the road, anticipating his son's appearance. And when he finally sees his son at a distance, he does it right. From reunion to restoration, this is one man who will not allow past disappointments to alter present determination.

2. Practice and teach the optimistic "faith view" that every problem can be solved by following God's plan.

The young man across from me had contemplated suicide on more than one occasion, and now he was recovering from a failed attempt. What had brought him to such a point of hopelessness? He opened up his heart enough for me to see what I believe was the real problem. Sure, he was in trouble at school, at home, and with the law. His troubles revolved, it seemed, around an unconquerable moral issue. But others have been in similar situations, or worse, and not attempted to bring an end to their life. What was his problem really?

This young man had been shortchanged of a vital piece of equipment absolutely necessary for facing the exigencies of life. He had never embraced the truth that every problem can be solved by following God's plan. So now, as far as he could see, he was in a situation from which there was no escape apart from death.

While we visited, he just casually mentioned something which I believe was at the root of his difficulty. As he continued to talk, my mental brakes came to a screeching halt when he said, "And that was the day my dad said he was through with me, that he had tried everything and had nothing else to offer. He said that nobody with my kind of problems ever got them solved. We really haven't talked much since then."

Nothing so devastates the spirit of a child as the belief that some problems just simply have no solution. It is not the father's responsibility always to have the answer to every problem. However, it is his responsibility to communicate this simple truth: Every problem can be resolved by finding and following God's plan. Without this understanding, a person can quickly sink into a life of despair and hopelessness.

At his worst moment in life, the prodigal son "came to himself" (Luke 15:17). He remembered his home, the place where he ought to be. No! Actually it was the place where he could be if he would simply follow God's plan of confession and repentance. "I have sinned against heaven, and before thee" (Luke 15:18). The greatest lesson taught by his father, the lesson that brought the son back home, was that every problem can be resolved by following God's plan.

3. Build into your family a sense of godly principle.

This is another element of the prodigal's return that is often overlooked. Listen again to the speech he first rehearsed then repeated to his father: "I . . . am no more worthy to be called thy son" (Luke 15:21). Do you see it? The family name stood for something. It was a name that was associated with the kind of godly principle he had rejected in his rebellion.

I am blessed by the legacy of faith left to me by all of my grandparents. My grandfather (on my mother's side) was a farmer, a county judge, and most importantly, the faithful father of eleven children. What's more, as they say in Bradly County, Arkansas, there was not a

cull in the bunch. Like their father and mother, these children have
lived out their lives, leaving a legacy of godliness and faith.

During my first two years of college, I had the privilege of pastoring a small mission church near my grandfather's farm where
I stayed over the weekends. I remember one of my aunts saying,
"Tommy, your grandfather has a name that stands for integrity. You
could go borrow money on his name alone. Don't mess it up!" Was
that a little pressure, or what?

One evening, my grandfather was reminiscing about the days
before the turn of the last century. He told how, riding home late one
evening, a masked bandit sprang from beside the road, pulled him off
his horse, and attempted to rob him at gunpoint. My grandfather put
up a fight, wrestled the pistol away from the man, threw him to the
ground, and pulled off his mask. Much to his surprise, the would-be
thief was an acquaintance who lived in the community.

My grandfather related that he talked with the man while seated
on his chest and looking down into his eyes. He told the man that if
he ever needed anything, he should simply ask. He elicited a promise
that he would never attempt such a thing again. "If you will keep that
promise," said my grandfather, "then I will not turn you in, and I will
never reveal your identity."

"That was years ago," said my grandfather. "In fact, the man has been
dead many years." "Who was he?" I asked. Looking at me with surprise,
my grandfather said, "Why, I told him I would never tell." The conversation was ended but not without my understanding that his name stood
for something. It was associated with godliness and principle.

Every father has the responsibility of passing on a good name,
which is to be chosen over great riches (Prov. 22:1). Your good
name, a name associated with godly principle, is of greater value than
anything of material wealth you might leave to your children.

4. Set the standard for forgiving.

The mental picture most of us paint when hearing this parable is
that of the father running to his son, embracing him, and welcoming
him home in an incredible display of forgiveness. The father did not
compromise good judgment by bailing the son out of his difficulties.
Neither did the restoration of his place as a son recover what the years

had wasted. Yet you cannot help being impressed by the father's forgiving spirit.

I'm not sure we would have handled the reunion in a similar fashion. Our tendency is to make people pay for their foolishness, heaping injury on injustice. "Look at him," we might have said, "that sniveling, wasted excuse for a son. That's it! Crawl! Let's see if you've learned your lesson. Come here, elder son, and witness what happens to a foolish rebel. Out on the porch, servants! Didn't I tell you he'd come back begging?"

Instead, the father races to his son, embraces him, hears part of his confession but never allows him to finish. All is forgiven! Does this mean the father approved of the sin? No. Does this mean the son will not suffer the loss of what was given him? No, it is already gone and cannot be recovered. It simply means he is forgiven and restored to a renewed relationship with his father. As a matter of fact, the father appears to have already forgiven him in his heart and just to be waiting for the son's return and repentance so that he could personally express his forgiveness.

A man was once asked if his children would be spending the holidays with him. "Not a chance," he growled. Then he proceeded to tell what a disappointment they had been to him. "We got into it one night," he told me, "over the details of their mother's funeral. They wanted one thing; I wanted another. Finally I told them that if that's what they wanted, they could just do it their way and pay for it themselves. That's what happened, and I've never forgiven them."

What was that man's legacy? At his death sometime later, his children remembered nothing except his unforgiveness. And, of course, their own unforgiving spirit was a testimony that he had effectively imprinted that legacy on them.

I have a friend who says that when an offense occurs, his goal is to "beat everyone to the foot of the cross." That is simply his way of saying that he wants to respond to offenses with a forgiving spirit. "Father, forgive them!" said Jesus while on the cross. Like your Heavenly Father, you ought to be the easiest person in your family to approach for forgiveness and the quickest to forgive.

5. *Do not dwell on past mistakes.*

While speaking of forgiving, it is important to recall that the Lord puts our sins behind him and remembers them no more. This contrasts with vivid recall that some fathers use when seeking to add emphasis to their admonitions. As one child said, "With my dad you don't ever just get a lecture; you get a life history."

The evidence in the parable is that the father resisted such a temptation. As the son begins to recount his sin and sorrow, his father calls for a robe, a ring, and shoes. Or as someone has said, "His daddy squealed, danced a reel, and cut the veal!" A review of his sins, especially on a continued basis, would have indicated that his forgiveness was in question because the father was unwilling to forget them. It would have made home an unhappy place to be since, after all, he was a constant trouble and a continued source of disappointment to his parents.

Children deserve to sense that some progress is being made along the path toward adulthood. Can you imagine how defeating it is to hear, "Well, here are the keys to the car. I hope you take better care of it than you did that bicycle I gave you in the sixth grade. Every time I go into the garage I see that twisted wreck just hanging there. I worry about you. I guess we'll just see how you do." A little more of that and you've got a teen whose mental bags are packed for the far country—just as far away as he can get, by the way.

"Your room is always dirty." "You are never on time." "You don't ever try." "You never show me any respect." "You're always just lazy around here." "These are no different from the grades you always get." "Those friends are no better than that last bunch." "And you never say you're sorry!" (Why should they? It doesn't seem to change the lecture or the life history.)

Aren't you glad the Lord doesn't review all your past failures, even the repeated ones, every time you come to him for forgiveness? Contemporary musician, Morgan Cryer, expresses the truth of God's love in a song that portrays a believer standing before God, grieving over sins committed while on earth. The title of the song is, "What Sins?" That pretty well sums up the truth of this fifth commandment.

6. Go out of your way to ensure family harmony and unity.

Sometimes we forget that there are actually two prodigal sons in this parable. The first becomes a prodigal through his actions, the second by his attitude. You will recall that the elder son remained faithfully at home seeking the best interests of his father. Imagine his surprise when, upon hearing music and laughing coming from his father's house, he is told that a welcome party is being thrown for his rebellious brother.

The elder son became upset over the situation and went out to the barn to throw a party for himself—a pity party. But his absence is noticed by his father! You can almost hear the back door closing softly and the voice of the father in the darkness, "Son! Son! Are you out here?" Gently he makes his case for welcoming the prodigal home.

He didn't have to do that, you know. He could have sent a servant to tell him to get inside, pronto! Or he could have said, "That's his tough luck! If he wants to be that way, he'll just miss a good time." Or he could have gone out and, without discussion, delivered a little lecture of his own. He did none of the above. What he did indicates his determination to ensure family unity.

To be perfectly frank, I have met fathers who are more childish than their children. They play favorites. They put one child against another. They allow family grievances to go unchallenged and unresolved. They really do not care whether their children have a good relationship. And woe be to the child who becomes the black sheep. He (or she) becomes the topic of every reunion.

Our Heavenly Father is jealous for the unity of his family. We are to love one another. We are known by our love. As for difficulties (which certainly arise), we are not to let the sun go down on our anger (Eph. 4:26). Nor are we to make an offering without first seeking to resolve any issue a brother might have against us. Our Father is big on the fellowship of love in the bond of peace.

A godly father will do no less in promoting harmony and peace in his own home. It will, as in this parable, often require that you go out of your way. It means that, as in this parable, you will sometimes be called to set aside your own interest and agenda to resolve a difficulty. It means that, as your children grow, they will understand from you that a bad attitude is just as much a cause for discipline as a bad action—maybe more so! It means that, ultimately, your family becomes a place of peace and harmony because you will not allow it to be otherwise.

Does it require time and effort to ensure harmony and unity? You bet! But the quicker you start the more your family will be blessed. Your home will really be a great place to live when growing up and to return frequently when you're grown.

7. Make certain that you positively respond to proper behavior.

A counselor of delinquent children once shared an interesting fact with me. She told me that, more than almost anything, children live for their father's approval. She told me what a real challenge this is for single moms or in families where the father is absent for extended periods of time. It's a simple fact that children don't just need their father's attention; they cannot thrive without it.

My counselor friend told me further that children so desperately need attention they will do anything to get it. "Negative behavior deserving severe discipline," she said, "will be incited by children who do not receive positive encouragement. In their hearts severe discipline is better than no attention at all."

For any of us, lack of attention indicates a lack of worth. It says, "You don't mean anything to me." That is why a father must think carefully about the kind of attention he gives his family. How often have you heard someone say in a fit of exasperation, "I never hear anything from you unless I do something wrong."

When the father left the party of prodigal number one to attend the party of prodigal number two, he took time to brag on the pouting elder son. "You have stuck with me," he said, "and as a result, everything I have is yours, not your brother's." In other words he was saying, "What you are and have done has not gone unnoticed. He gets a party. Your positive behavior is rewarded with everything I have. Loosen up! Take a good look at the way things are. I think you'll like what you see."

When you think about it, both sons were receiving a positive response for proper behavior. The younger son received restoration for his repentance. The elder received a farm and a fortune for his faithfulness. No wonder the father is really the hero in this story!

8. Deal with your children according to their God-given personalities.

Each one of us is different from all others. (Praise the Lord!) Some of those differences are the result of external elements (environment, experiences, etc.). Other differences are evidences that God creates each of us with unique personalities. This is why different people respond to similar circumstances in different ways.

If you fail to understand this simple principle, you will not be able to understand the behavior of the father in our parable. Why would he refuse to go after one son whose behavior carried him far away yet go out to the other who was merely sitting in the barn? The answer is simple: He understood each of his sons. He knew that each would respond differently to circumstances. The younger would have to experience total loss before returning home. The elder son would respond to the gentle reason of a loving lecture.

"I don't know why that child has turned away from our family and God," I've heard some folks lament. "After all, we raised them all the same." Oh, there's the problem. You were attempting the impossible. Parenting is an art, not a science. Children cannot be pressed into the same mold. No child is the same as another child. Attempting to raise each child in the same manner will cause your children to be frustrated. One of the most disappointing experiences in life will come with the discovery that you just can't raise them all the same.

Knowing something about trees will help you here. There are vast differences between an oak tree and a willow. Actually, you can make an oak grow like a drooping willow by using constant restraint. Just drive stakes in the ground, tie lines to the limbs of the oak, and pull them down. It will look like a willow, sort of. But it's not a willow. And it will be constantly working against the restraints. Once the restraints are broken, or unloosed, that tree will go right back to growing like an oak.

Like those trees, each of us has our God-given personality. One of the great challenges to a father is finding that bent and seeking to bring it under the loving hand of God. What appears to be recklessness can, by God's grace, become boldness. Impulsiveness can become decisiveness; stubbornness can become perseverance. That is why the

writer of Proverbs tells us that a child trained in the way he should go
(that is, with an understanding of his God-given personality) will,
when grown, be able to withstand the storms of life.

But this can only happen IF you are willing to take the time truly
to know your child, something many fathers never get around to
doing. It takes time to talk, listen, observe, pray. You won't always get
it right. But remember, your children are God's homework assignment to you. So get to work.

**9. Do not overlook golden opportunities to teach scriptural
principles.**

What an aggravation! Rather than allow my daughter's "friend" to
bring her home after the game, I was driving the sixteen-mile round trip
to pick her up at school. I had no good reason for doing so, just a feeling. She had faithfully followed the drill through the early months of
her junior year in high school. Go to the game on the school bus. Ride
it back to the school. Call from the school. Then go with her friend to
drink a Coke before coming home. Simple! Trouble free! And she had
done exactly as agreed. Now here I was balking at the arrangement.

There was a "chill on the meeting" as we drove from the school.
I was trying to explain why I had come to get her, but I was getting
nowhere. Finally I just leveled with her. "Beth," I said, "it's nothing
either of you has done. I am your father and am assigned the role of
your protector until you are married. I don't know why I feel this way,
but I do! And I cannot put it aside simply because it's illogical. It must
be enough that it's in my heart, and you must trust me." She was
blowing frost on the window of the passenger side.

We drove home without another word, parked the car, and walked
into the house. The phone was ringing, and Beth went to answer it.
I noticed her face turn pale as she listened, then hung up the receiver.

"Daddy," she said, "that was Jeff calling from the hospital emergency room. As he drove from the school parking lot, someone shot a
rifle bullet through the passenger window of his car. "Oh daddy," she
sobbed, "if I had been with him, it would have hit me. I promise I will
never again question your decisions regarding me." This was a huge
lesson neither of us had anticipated. But it was a lesson that would

have been lost (and perhaps her life with it) had I not unwittingly been willing to take the time and effort required to share it.

The father didn't simply talk with the elder son about the return of the prodigal. He used the time to share with him about the rewards of faithfulness. Never overlook a golden, God-given opportunity to teach a scriptural principle.

10. Be home when they come home.

Can you imagine how the prodigal would have responded if upon his return there had been no father to welcome him. "Sorry, son. You're Dad said things were just too rough around here. All his work kept him so busy we had little time for ourselves. The marriage fell apart, and he's gone. But that's life, as they say. You'll get over it!"

More than half of the children in America's public schools live in single-parent homes. One-third of those will never set foot in the home of their biological father. These children have a 300 percent greater possibility of a negative life outcome (crime, drugs, sexual promiscuity, and divorce) than those reared in two-parent families. Even if their wayward children came home, their fathers would not be there to greet them.

There is something incredibly stabilizing about a home where father and mother are committed "until death do us part." There are enough questions in life without children having to ask, "Where's Dad?" Or worse, "Who is my dad?" In some parts of our society, children do not know the meaning of the question, What is your home address? But they do respond to, Where are you staying now?

When we pray, it is not to get the attention of our Heavenly Father. He's there! We have his attention. Children deserve the same of their earthly fathers, their "picture of God." They should not have to wonder where, or who, he is. This last commandment for fathers is the easiest to understand. No discussion needed. Dad, be there when they get there.

PART TWO

From the Children to Their Parents

Seeking and Obeying
Tending Your Marriage
Consumed, but with Whom?
Trying Times

*W*hat started out as an afterthought has ended up providing what, for many of you, will be the most significant part of this book. We asked our children to respond with letters of their own, letters which we hoped would serve as living examples of the truths we have sought to impart to them over the years. We were overwhelmed by their response. In fact, we still wonder if this book should not be titled, *Letters to Parents*, with our meager contribution listed in the appendix!

In these chapters you will read about the significance of finding God's direction and doing it; the importance of tending to your marriage; the confidence of a parent's love enabling children to respond to discipline; and how each generation is experiencing their own trying times.

When these letters were written, we had been married only thirty-six years. These have been exhilarating years seeming to demand a new exercise of faith at every turn. We always rejoice when some couple is introduced in our church as having been married sixty years or more. Afterward, we secretly agree to beat their record!

OK kids, give us your best shot!

CHAPTER NINE

Seeking and Obeying

Dear Dad and Mom,

It is hard for us to believe that we are heading into our fifteenth year of marriage. Little did we realize, standing at the marriage altar, that we were embarking on the most incredible years of our lives.

The whole romantic notion of falling in love and planning our future together seemed, at the time, enough to carry us through anything we would ever face. Yet before us was a whole world filled with new struggles, unexpected joys, great challenges, and life-changing choices.

As we began our life together, your unconditional love and constant enthusiasm for what God was doing in our lives became a major contributor to the nature of our relationship. This built the confidence in us that we needed, for standing alone as a couple before the Lord is a beautiful change yet not without its trials. How thankful we are to you for pushing us out that door, encouraging us to cleave to each other and seek God's will for our own lives.

At first we found ourselves timid to believe that God could direct us without specific counsel from you as our parents. On many occasions we would come to you and ask, "What should we do?" We are certain there were times you would have rather pointed us in the direction you felt was safest based on your own experiences. However, you were faithful to direct us to the Lord. "Go to the Lord," you would both say. "Ask him what you should do."

Not only did you say this, but you also lived this in front of us. As we watched you make decisions based on God's direction rather than man's opinion, we began to see that God does not have a canned answer for any aspect of our lives.

The real choices boil down to two simple questions. (1) Are we willing to seek God's will on an issue? (2) When we find His will, are we willing to obey Him?

Thank you, Dad and Mom, for showing us the blessings of following this process, the process of seeking God and obeying Him. We love you.

Tony and Beth

The issues that blaze themselves through the Christian sky are here one minute and gone the next. At any moment the depth of our spirituality seems to be measured by the choices we make in our marriage concerning whatever is the "hottest" Christian topic. These issues send husbands and wives battling back and forth, desiring God's will but more focused on "what others might think."

Many times we feel it would make things so much easier if we could just follow what someone else claims to be God's way. We trust that surely others have sought the Lord and his will must be the same for all. Yet God's Word constantly warns us of the dangers in following after man's approval instead of God's specific plan for our life. "The fear of man brings a snare, But he who trusts in the LORD will be exalted" (Prov. 29:25 NASB).

Now fifteen years into marriage, God has seen fit to bless us with eight children. The importance of our choices now affects not just our own lives but eventually the lives of many, many people. Having a large family offers certain opportunities. People assume you must really have a handle on things and tend to ask advice on all sorts of issues. We are asked about all kinds of topics from birth control, homeschooling versus Christian or public schooling, child rearing, music, youth group involvement, to dating and marriage communication. We would like to be able to claim that we have a grasp on all of these issues, but that would be a lie.

The reality is that sometimes we want to wear shirts that say, "We are normal; we just have all these children living with us." Have you ever awakened with the thought, *What in the world are we doing here, and what do we do next?* We have. Our marriage has seen days of overwhelming situations, crises of faith, financial burdens, cumbersome responsibilities, and life-changing decisions. Anything we are able to share in this chapter is only by the grace of God and most likely learned through our own failures. Those daily struggles have drawn us to desire his way more deeply and not our own. Therefore we have more easily come to welcome His reminders to seek Him!

The path of seeking the Lord on both small and big issues has shown us a beautiful truth. God will speak to us just as He did to great men and women of the Bible such as Moses, Joseph, Daniel, Esther, and Mary. Not only this but He also has incredible and unbelievable blessings in store for those who seek Him. "Now unto him that is able to do exceeding abundantly above all that we ask or think, according to the power that worketh in us" (Eph. 3:20). So, exactly how do you seek God?

SEEKING GOD

"I love those who love me; and those who diligently seek me will find me" (Prov. 8:17 NASB). Our Heavenly Father is not in the business of trying to keep his will from us. He does desire that we earnestly seek Him, but it is His pleasure to show us the right path and the victory. We can be confident that if we do seek Him, we will find Him.

The first step in seeking the Lord is establishing a relationship with Him. People generally do not share personal issues with someone with whom they did not first have a relationship. God offers this to us freely. We can become his children by making a decision of trust. By realizing we are hopeless without God and deserving of death for our sin, we can accept God's forgiveness and his free gift of life by simply trusting in one thing. By choosing to believe that God's own son Jesus died on the cross as a payment for our sin and the death that we deserved, we can receive the gift of being called God's child as well as an eternity in heaven when we die. "For God so loved the world that He gave His only begotten Son, that whosoever believes in Him should not perish but have everlasting life" (John 3:16 NKJV) Who loves to give advice the most? Parents of course! So what better relationship to establish than the one of being God's child!

Maintaining a relationship with the Lord is the next step in "seeking" Him. However, this takes self-discipline and commitment. Talking to Him daily (prayer) and hearing from Him daily (reading God's Word, the Bible) keeps your relationship open and intimate. Just as your own child cannot ever become "not your child," once accepting Christ, you will forever be His. However, this does not keep your relationship close without a little effort.

God meets with each of us differently. Finding time to spend with the Lord in the morning is a wonderful encouragement, and it can begin your day with his perspective rather than your own. On many occasions we have found that in our morning times with the Lord, He has been able to prepare us for some choice or situation that lies just ahead. If you have young children, you may feel as if you have to sleep in your running shoes in order to keep up with your life. Do not be discouraged if establishing a consistent time each day is an ongoing struggle. "He shall feed his flock like a shepherd: he shall gather the lambs with his arm, . . . and shall gently lead those that are with young" (Isa. 40:11).

Our experience is that when your home is filled with young children, both partners, but especially the wives, truly struggle finding even a moment to breathe much less a quiet time where they are not crashing into bed. During these days when the wife feels emotionally and physically drained, it helps when the husband makes sure he is reaching out to his wife and encouraging her spiritually. This could even be reading the Bible out loud to her as she is falling asleep or at the side of the bed before he heads to work. Sometimes it may be sharing only what God is showing Him. We have found encouragement from sharing Scriptures with each other. Your time with the Lord may never be picture perfect; nevertheless, finding time for your relationship with the Lord is a must, and if God's will for the choices of your life are important, then it must be a priority.

You choose to get up every morning. Why not commit never to let your head hit the pillow without spending some time with Him. Hopefully most of those times will be in the morning and with enough time to pour out your heart and let Him pour into you through His Word. Some days this will mean reading several verses as you fall into bed. While this isn't the best way to get any huge answers, remember He gently leads those with young and is not an unmerciful God disowning you because you didn't clock in the right amount of minutes. The key in maintaining a relationship is keeping your heart close to Him.

As a couple, hold each other accountable, check up on each other's relationship with the Lord, not with criticism but with interest in hearing what the other is finding from the Lord. Remember to make your decisions together with Him. If you are struggling to find time to speak to your spouse, go for a walk in the evenings. There have been times that to have a good conversation with each other we have run to a restaurant less than a mile from our home, or fed the kids early and put them to bed so we could eat together and talk alone. Spend time talking so that you seek God together.

This leads to the next step in "seeking." When you are dealing with something specific or needing direction, ask specifically and ask together! When you go to the Lord, you need not beat around the bush with all sorts of spiritual jargon. As God and your Father, He is fully aware of your needs, so don't be afraid to be honest and forthright.

Early in our marriage we faced a medical decision that would place us without a doctor three days before our child was due to be born. It was our first big crisis! Were we willing to seek the Lord on this? All we knew to say was, "Lord, what do we do today?" Standing on a sliver of faith, we called to the Lord and went to His Word wondering how God could give us specific direction regarding this immediate and detailed situation. He did not leave us hanging but gave us clear directions in His Word! Even though we did not know exactly what lay ahead, we knew what we were asked to do. Then came the next choice. We obeyed, and God of course was faithful. Almost immediately we were placed under the care of an incredibly godly doctor who became not only the trusted hands God used to bring our child into the world but a lifelong friend!

Once you have felt the peace in your heart, once you step out in faith to obey God and find on the other side His faithfulness and blessing, you will also find strength to follow this process again. Your next trial and decision may be just around the corner as ours were.

Another part of "seeking" is listening. This can be done in several ways. You can gather counsel from one or two sources of godly men and women. We have been so blessed to have both sets of parents nearby to ask advice. We have also learned another valuable truth from them: Regardless of the counsel you may offer to others, it is important to always remind them that, ultimately, they must seek the Lord. When requested, our parents offer us their counsel, reminding us, "You need to make sure that the Lord verifies what we have said. His ways are above our ways and He may have a different plan. So be certain that what we have said is consistent with God's Word."

If you do not have the privilege of living with a godly family influence nearby, seek to surround yourself with friends who will encourage you to follow after the Lord. You can also look for people whom you notice are leaders in their fields but have an obvious walk with the Lord.

Another way to listen is to be attentive in the church services you attend. As you attend a church where God's Word is taught, you can take comfort in knowing that God uses His servants to feed and encourage those under His leading. God may also use times of fellowship with other believers, a time of worship, or a specific song to encourage you to continue in obedience. God will be faithful to lead you so watch and listen.

Let us clarify that the Lord will never ask you to do something that goes against obvious biblical principles. For instance, the Bible states, "Thou shalt not steal" (Exod. 20:15). If you are going to the Lord and asking whether you should steal, you are asking a question that already has an answer.

Listen to God as you read His Word. Asking God for a specific passage of Scripture to give you direction is a practice we highly recommend. As always our emotions can change, and finding a verse you can cling to can bring such confidence when being obedient is not easy. His word is alive. It is written for each of us as well as all of us.

Prior to purchasing some property, we went to the Lord asking for a confirmation in His Word to make this decision. He just would not let us move forward. We continued to wait and ultimately received a word saying that this was not God's will for us. As discouraging as this was, we obeyed, and only six months later God led us to our new home. It was so much more than what we had hoped for.

Many people are hesitant to believe that God will speak to them through His Word and feel this is "only for ministers." This just isn't so. We tend to be afraid to attempt this out of fear over several things. We are either afraid we will not hear from Him and be disappointed, afraid that His answer will not be what we desire, afraid that we will misunderstand, or afraid that we will not be able to do as He says.

These fears are completely unfounded, for He says if we seek Him, He will be found. Jeremiah 29:11 tells us that His plans are to prosper us and not Harm us; He promises us that even though we may stumble, we will "not be utterly cast down" (Ps. 37:24), and if He asks something of us, He will give us the grace to be obedient!

So once we have found His will in an issue, we can only face the next decision. Are we willing to obey Him? And just how do we obey?

OBEDIENCE

Unlike our last question, there are not multitudes of avenues of obedience. Parents find themselves frustrated with children who want to obey but want to do it "their way." Unfortunately this is not just common in children but common in all sinners. Perhaps we feel our way will be better, easier, and maybe safer. From our experience we would like to encourage you not to try this road. It is a dead end. God actually does know best.

With the question of obedience, there is truly only one choice. Once you have heard from God, either you will obey or you will disobey. There is no middle road with God. Of course obedience to God does not always yield an approval from man, and this is something most people hate to face.

Obedience is an issue of faith. When you obey, you are saying to God and to others, "This may not seem right and may not gain us approval in man's eyes, but in trust we are choosing to believe that God knows best, and we desire to please Him no matter the sacrifice."

In preparation for obedience, your time with the Lord can build great confidence. Filling your mind with His Word can flex those trust muscles, but when it comes down to it, the way you obey is just like the Nike slogan, "Just do it!"

Not long ago we faced a decision we had avoided for some time. After being asked to be involved in several different things at our church, we went to the Lord for some direction. With both of us being raised in the church, we were accustomed to being involved in just about everything the church and our local private school had to offer. As we began to look at our home, our relationships with our immediate family, and our relationship with those around us who didn't know Christ, we realized something was wrong. While we were busy with so many good and spiritual activities, we were failing at what God requires of us.

Upon seeking the Lord, He began to convict us of a common trap in our culture. We were so busy being involved and keeping up appearances that we were failing at what God called us to do. We began making new decisions, and with each one, analyzing if this choice would truly help us reach our calling as a couple.

Through this process we began eliminating many of the things we loved but that were stealing time from our home. We began to turn our focus towards our home and found the rewards immeasurable.

Of course there have been times when others have not understood. We have not regretted our decisions however, because the rewards have far outweighed the struggles of facing others' approval. One of the questions we ask when adding or removing activities is, "Will this add to the peace of our home?" Sometimes the busyness of an activity will in the long run add to the peace, and yet many times it will not.

The reality is that raising a family takes time! Having a relationship with a spouse takes time! Having a relationship with the Lord takes time! Contrary to popular opinion, these priorities require quantity time not just quality time.

This means dads actually must spend time with their children where there is no other distraction and opportunity to communicate. We have found that involving our children in golf provides a great amount of time to communicate. On vacations we spend time fishing. Of course our fishing experiences with six to eight children are not always textbook. We are usually scaring the fish away with so much noise, yet we do catch uninterrupted time with our kids.

This means that moms must not be afraid to say, "For the next several days, we are going to hang out with one another instead of our friends. It also means that we will not be able to be involved in every sport, every camp, every party, and every opportunity that arises. All things good for us are not necessarily best for us."

To protect our time together as a couple, we have to find time alone as well. This may mean that in church we find a place to minister together. This may mean that we are unable to attend some meetings. We must be responsible to stay aware of the barometer of our home. By continually watching the atmosphere of our home, we more easily seek God's guidance on the real issues facing us.

While attempting to regain some ground in our home, we found that God was working on our hearts. He began to expose what was really in us. Were we seeking Him with all our heart or seeking others? Were we seeking His will or our own? What was the motivating factor behind our choices? Was it our desire to become more like Christ and be an example of His love, or was it our selfishness?

What we found was that we were a couple completely consumed by our desire to please God while making a great impression on others. We had so much pride. God has now been working on us for fifteen years, showing us the wisdom of His will and the sacrifice we must make in order to be obedient.

Only months ago we entered into another desperate cry to the Lord about a decision we needed to make regarding our children's schooling. We discussed and battled back and forth the emotions of how our decision would affect our children. Well-meaning friends offered opinions that sent us reeling with desire for man's approval. When it came down to the line, we knew where we must turn.

Are we willing once again to seek the Lord on another issue?

Are we willing to obey Him?

Our answer is an emphatic yes, for we know this will bring us peace. What will you do?

CHAPTER TEN

Tending Your Marriage

Dear Dad and Mom,

As we think about marriage and what lessons we have learned, there are so many valuable truths that we have learned along the way from you. Thank you for your example to us concerning the priority of marriage. Thank you for showing us that a marriage is something to be guarded, cared for tenderly, and tended. You have carefully tended to your relationship as husband and wife in some significant ways for us to see. Having been married now for almost eight years, we can see what a priceless picture you have placed before us, showing us not just what to do to tend our marriage but how to do it. Thank you for giving us the opportunity to observe your relationship and see what it means to treasure each other.

One thing that sticks out to us is the way you laugh together and try to find the humorous side of things with each other. You rarely allow a situation to weigh you down so much that you cannot laugh.

It has been fun to recount the story of a long family road trip. Everyone was hungry and dying to find a drive-through and grab something to eat. But you, Dad, were a man on a mission and didn't want to waste time. As the car passed the last exit available for miles, Mom cried out, "Tom, what are we going to do?" Well, then, you started into a round:

> *What are we going to do, Mama?*
> *What are we going to do?*
> *What are we going to do, Mama?*
> *What are we going to do?*

Half the family began to chime in, while the other half chanted in rhythm,

> *Whatever will we do?*
> *Whatever will we do?*
> *Whatever will we do?*

The family did this in a round and just roared with laughter, traveling down the road to uncertain hunger and starvation. It's funny how we have found ourselves doing things like this now with our family, making up silly rhymes about things at times.

Another way we see that you both tend your marriage relationship is through the time you are careful to spend with each other. We know you spend time together in the morning praying and talking about the day, and your yearly getaway to Hawaii says volumes to us about how you value each other and want to be with each other alone, in order to cultivate your marriage.

Thank you also for caring for your relationship by forgiving each other. We know that you have a habit of never going to sleep at night with any sort of disagreement between you. That is something we have purposed to do in our own marriage. You also show kindness toward each other in your speech. We never hear you talking harshly or curtly toward each other. Amy has commented often that yelling was not an option in the household in which she grew up; it was too demeaning and hurtful. We know that you are always committed to getting together alone if there is something you need to settle or discuss.

We have also seen you carefully cultivate the garden of your love relationship by making your relationship with God a priority. Dad, we know you are a man of prayer. Amy has often spoken of seeing you countless times reading and studying the Word, walking into your study to find you bowing before the Lord. Even on our big family vacations, sometimes with all five families and eighteen children together, you always find some time in the early morning hours or during the day to steal away with your Bible and perhaps a cup of coffee to be still before the Lord.

Mom, you have also been such an example to us of faithfulness in your study of the Word and prayer. With five children now of our own, we are both well aware of the challenges of taking time to be alone with God each day. We can see that the key to your happy, healthy marriage—and any happy, healthy marriage—is a central daily walk with God: being in the Word, worshiping, praying. We're working to follow this example!

Thank you for tending to your marriage by serving God together. You don't separate and go your own ways. Your agenda has always meshed together. You really have a one-flesh ministry. Mom, you are so involved in all Dad does; and Dad, you involve Mom. We see you, Mom, as such a picture of service, and it's obvious that both you and Dad are so fulfilled in your ministry together to others. We are learning to see now why a healthy, godly marriage is not a worthy goal in and of itself. There is a more wonderful goal in it all. We are seeing that unless we ourselves, in our marriage and in our family, are seeking to carry out the purposes of God, our marriage and home fall short of what God intended.

Thank you, Dad and Mom, for the lessons you have shown to us as a couple. Thank you for helping us to start out right. Marriage is the

*most wonderful experience of our lives. Thank you for praying for us
as we seek carefully to tend the garden of our marriage. May it bear
much fruit and truly honor Him.*
Love,
David and Amy

We have said many times that our favorite thing about being married is the companionship we enjoy. The romance is great. Having children is a wonderful journey we are taking together. Working together, serving together, and fulfilling our God-ordained roles yields incredible pleasures. But nothing is more satisfying in marriage than sweet intimate friendship.

In the 1828 *Dictionary of the English Language,* Noah Webster said:

> But when thou findest sensibility of heart, joined with softness of manners; an accomplished mind and religion, united with sweetness of temper, modest deportment, and a love of domestic life—such is the woman who will divide the sorrows, and double the joys of thy life. Take her to thyself; she is worthy to be thy nearest friend, thy companion, the wife of thy bosom.

Webster discovered the fulfillment of companionship with his wife. He experienced and believed in the joy of friendship in marriage. He saw the "fitted-ness" of two people God placed together in a marriage relationship.

When we first met, I (Amy) was not struck with love at first sight; but maybe it was "like" at first sight. Before David, I had never met an individual that I just wanted to be around. He made me laugh. He was interested in what I said. We clicked. I thought to myself, the first night I met him, *I want to be his friend. I really want to get to know this man.* What a privilege was mine to be able to do that! Eight days after he moved into town, he asked me out, and things moved pretty quickly after that.

It was apparent to us on our first date that God took pleasure in and was blessing our relationship. It was good for us to be with each other, and we sensed Him smiling on us, paving the way for us to have a permanent relationship.

A husband cannot replace a wife's need for sharpening female friendships, nor can a wife replace a husband's need for men who will run the race beside him and challenge him spiritually. Our marriage relationship is the most significant relationship of this life!

When we were dating, I (David) had a dream. I don't take much stock in dreams, but this dream was particularly meaningful. In the dream I was running a cross-country race, and Amy was running it with me. Amy fell, and when she did, I came back to help her get up, overcome the soreness, and go on to finish the race together. That is the picture of companionship in marriage. God has placed us in this race together. We need each other. "Two are better than one. . . . For if either of them falls, the one will lift up his companion" (Eccles. 4:9–10 NASB).

If we are to maintain our companionship in marriage, we must nurture and tend our relationship. Just as any other friendship only grows by communication and attention, so the marriage relationship must be tended. I sometimes call David my "husbandman." The word *husband* comes from the word *husbandman*. A husbandman is a caretaker of a garden, a vineyard, an estate. David is a husbandman to me. He takes care of me. And I am made for him, to be a helpmeet for him.

Genesis 2 says that among all the cattle and birds and beasts there was not a helper suited for Adam.

> So the LORD God caused a deep sleep to fall upon the man, and he slept; then He took one of his ribs and closed up the flesh at that place. The LORD God fashioned into a woman the rib which He had taken from the man, and brought her to the man. The man said, "This is now bone of my bones, and flesh of my flesh; She shall be called woman, because she was taken out of Man." For this reason a man shall leave his father and his mother, and be joined to his wife; and they shall become one flesh (Gen. 2:21–24 NASB).

Eve was created as suitable for Adam and he for her. They were a perfect fit for each other mentally, emotionally, spiritually, and physically.

As married partners, we are in a unique, God-designed relationship. We are to cleave to each other in every way. Notice that the Scripture commands that to have the kind of relationship God intended, we have to both leave and cleave. Leave all other relationships in as much as they hinder us from our marriage relationship, and cleave to each other only. Our relationship becomes the priority relationship. It is more important than the relationship with our parents, or our children.

Because companionship is so important, we must tend to our relationship. It is like the first ten-by-ten-foot vegetable garden we had the first year we were married. We took such pride in that little plot! We kept it, weeded it, fertilized it, and watered it. We harvested the squash, tomatoes, carrots, and eggplant. (What do you do with three rows of eggplant?) As we became busy with other demands on our lives, we failed to cultivate and tend to that little garden. The squash quickly took over the garden, and soon the little neat rows could not be seen for all the squash vines.

We must care for our marriage companionship if it is to be healthy. We must tend it lovingly. We can take care of our marital relationship in many ways. We have found that some of the most important avenues to tending a marriage include laughing together, making time with each other a priority, forgiving each other, maintaining personal spiritual disciplines, and pursuing the purposes of God together.

TEND TO YOUR MARRIAGE BY LAUGHING AT LIFE TOGETHER

When we were on our honeymoon, we stayed for a short time at a luxurious hotel. We had a VIP suite at the top of the hotel with a panoramic view of the city, several rooms, two bathrooms, a small study, a kitchen. It was pretty fancy. We were impressed, anyway. As we came up from breakfast one morning, we were talking about our great room, and we figured it must have a name. All VIP suites generally have a special name on a plaque outside. As we neared the entry, David stopped short and proclaimed, "Honey, here it is." With a wide sweep of his hand, he gestured to the plaque on the wall, and said, "We are staying in the 'North Star.'" When Amy looked at the plaque, she began to chuckle. "Honey, that says 'North Stair.'" At that point all of our honeymoon nerves melted away, and we burst into the door of our room and fell on the floor laughing. It was a great way to start a honeymoon and a marriage—with laughter.

Humor can take a married couple a long way in stressful times. It is crucial to foster humor and laughter with each other and in a family to help in times like this.

Several years after we married, we sensed the Lord leading us to move to Cambodia, to do Great Commission work in that country. Preparing for the drastic changes ahead and packing up our lives was a stressful experience at times. We spent several days preparing forms, wills, and medical history questionnaires. One of the questions asked us to rate our overall physical condition, as either poor, fair, good, or vigorous. One evening, as we were drifting off to sleep, I suddenly thought of that question and asked David, "Sweetheart, what did you circle on the question rating your physical condition?" Silence. I got tickled. "Did you put 'vigorous'?" I asked. "What did you put?" he asked me, shaking with laughter. When it was finally out, we both confessed that we had rated ourselves as "vigorous," and we laughed and laughed until it hurt.

Just recently, after dinner one evening, our little daughter stood in front of the fireplace and said, "Come on everyone, come in here and dance with me." So all the rest of us gathered in front of Allie in the living room, facing her. We had to copy everything she was doing. Then the boys had to have a turn. It was such fun being silly together. After that, all the kids called for Daddy to get up on the fireplace and lead the dance, which he consented to do. He couldn't think of any other thing to do than sing "Boom-chutcha, boom-chutcha" and swing his hands about like a really bad cheerleader. We all got so tickled we could hardly continue. The kids still ask for Daddy to get up there and do his funny dance again.

Laughter is good. It is good for a marriage. It is good for your family. It is an important ingredient for a good marriage. Don't forget to laugh together!

TEND TO YOUR MARRIAGE BY SPENDING TIME TOGETHER

Probably the greatest solace we found in Cambodia is the joy of being with each other in the evenings after the kids are quiet and in their beds. In that culture our evenings are especially quiet and alone and meaningful because there is not a square box with channels that calls for our attention. The only way we keep up with world news in our little town of Siem Reap is through our shortwave radio. In the evenings we talk. We plan. We read. We sing. We watch a video together. We dream. For the past few years we have been planning a second honeymoon. We have had such fun talking about what we wanted to do, where we wanted to go, searching for different destinations. Honestly, half the fun was planning it together!

When we finally did go on that second honeymoon, it was such a wonderful time. We had planned it well and prepared for a great time. Now we have a whole handful of new and precious memories together.

While on our second honeymoon, we discussed many issues. David asked me some deep questions about me personally, about us, about our family. At the end of our time there, we made some resolutions for our marriage, and we are better for it. We have a better marriage because we tended to it. We tended it with time. We can't be friends or companions without spending time with each other.

For the past three years we have had a habit of having a date with each other every week. Because of our situation in Cambodia, it is not wise for us to go out at night, so we have a weekly "day date." Every Wednesday while someone watches our kids, we head off for two or three hours. Usually we go to a hotel where we can cool off in air-conditioning, a luxury we don't enjoy in our home. And there in that lovely hotel, we drink limeades, eat complimentary peanuts, and talk. Occasionally we go for a swim or out to lunch, or we find a hotel that has an English-language broadcast so we can catch up on what is happening in the world. Whatever we do, we prize those hours and look forward to them every week. Those times together are a midweek breather, something to readjust our thinking, times for us to pray and plan.

What else do we do together? We make great salsa. We like to watch old movies. We like to worship together (David on the guitar and Amy on the piano). Every couple has some unique likes and dislikes. It has taken us some time to discover what we enjoy doing together. I do not enjoy putting together photo albums with Amy—cutting out all those little squiggly lines and hearts to make it all pretty, and Amy does not enjoy sitting up in bed playing computer hunting games—using elk calls and tracking bear signs or dropping a big buck at three hundred yards. But we enjoy doing other things together. We are in the process of discovering those things. Why? Because we need to spend time together.

To make time with my spouse a priority means eliminating some other activities in our lives to allow space for each other, time for each other. Because we live in Cambodia, we don't have commitments at night. Cambodia is a Third World country with poor roads and no electricity in most rural areas. So when it is dark, people stay in and go to bed. There is not much going on at night, so every evening our family is together. And after the kids are down, we have time alone. Although we are busy during the day, we appreciate the slowing down at night in Cambodia. It allows us to tend to our marriage and family needs.

What does a wildly paced American couple do to spend time together? Many couples have commitments every night, constant obligations to fulfill. The answer lies in cutting out some of those "musts." Not everything can be a must. If the marriage relationship is priority, as the Word of God indicates, then some obligations must be declined. Simplify. It will do wonders for your marriage.

TEND TO YOUR MARRIAGE BY FORGIVING EACH OTHER

Forgiveness is laying down your right to be treated a certain way. That is why it is Christlike. It is what Christ did (Phil. 2:5–8). Forgiveness is essential, especially in marriage. The closer we come together, the more we see each other's faults and failures.

There was once a sweet older lady who had been happily married for many years. Someone asked her the secret to her happy, peaceful marriage. She revealed that she had made a list before she married of ten faults she would forgive and ignore in her husband, and as she forgave him these things, their marriage grew in love and forgiveness. When asked what the items on the list were, she answered, "I forgot!" What a precious picture of someone who through practicing forgiveness allowed that quality of Christ to become such a part of her.

Life in Cambodia can be crazy at times, with visitors dropping in unannounced from the countryside, running out of water, the electricity going off for hours on end, weird sicknesses, and a variety of other things. Learning to lay down your rights is a must. Not letting things build up is another must. We would be lying if we didn't admit that there are times when one of us is tired or frustrated and talks sharply to the other. At that point the other of us has an option—to overlook it and forgive or, after feelings have settled, to talk about it. We have committed not to let offenses build up but to deal with hurts quickly and lovingly before ill feelings are allowed to build up.

Sometimes couples play the silent game. They think that, by silence, they are punishing each other by withholding communication, love, or affection. Sometimes we see couples choose to lash out angrily at each other, bringing up offenses from the past. It's obvious that they do not practice forgiveness in their marriage, and the result is pain for both of them and for their children.

We have discovered that the key to keeping peace in our marriage is to keep our accounts short. When an offense occurs, forgive, or discuss and forgive. Never do we dare let our heads touch that pillow with anger or hurt festering. We know that issues can grow into monstrous proportions that way. In many marriages what starts out as such a small petty offense, left unresolved, becomes a huge problem that gets heavier and causes sharp, angry, ugly feelings to creep in.

Look what we have been forgiven of: everything—all of the evil and sin in our lives past, present, and future. The Word of God says that if we do not forgive, we will not be forgiven of God. "For if you forgive men their trespasses, your Heavenly Father will also forgive you. But if you do not forgive men their trespasses, neither will your Father forgive your trespasses" (Matt. 6:14–15 NKJV).

Because there are many hardships in life, we need each other desperately. The last thing in the world we need is to be at odds with each other. We're in this thing together forever, and that requires forgiving each other daily.

TEND TO YOUR MARRIAGE BY MAINTAINING A GROWING RELATIONSHIP WITH GOD

Our Heavenly Father will lovingly tend our marriage as we daily seek and worship Him. Keeping up with the disciplines of our faith can be hard to do as children come along and time pressures increase. It is a daily fight to squeeze in minutes alone with the Lord. Being alone with the Lord may not necessarily mean all alone. There may be children all around, or noise, or weariness overcoming us. There are always factors that are less than ideal. It is easy to toss out that time with God as different stresses build up in our lives. In times when we desperately need to seek the Lord and walk with Him, we are apt to move on without Him.

Several years ago our family was in Thailand for a conference with other missionaries in Southeast Asia. Amy was three months pregnant with our fourth child. While we were at the conference, she began to miscarry our baby. She was taken to the hospital where doctors determined that the baby was already dead. We were shocked. No one had ever had a miscarriage in our family before, and we were incredulous at what was happening to us. The grace of God became apparent immediately. Kind people were all around us. Good medical care was obtainable. Through our tears we instantly saw that God was good, and He was drawing us to Himself at that time.

Strangely, through this hard event, God pulled us ever so gently out of a creeping apathy of soul. We had become so dry, and there seemed to be simply memories of sweet times with the Lord. We were ever looking back. Nothing new or special was happening in our relationship with God at that time. We had both become inconsistent in the spiritual disciplines of studying the Word, praying, and worshiping.

I (Amy) knew that I had to start consistently spending time with the Lord again. I knew that I needed desperately to spend time in prayer with the Lord. I knew that I needed to study (not just read) His Word. I knew that worship had to become a part of my day again. I knew it was going to be a challenge to do all these things, but God was with me in it.

I ended up carving the oddest time out of my day to spend with God, but it worked. In the middle of the morning, I put my youngest down for a nap. Then I would have my two oldest play in their room. I would sit down in the living room with my Bible, journal, prayer record, and a hymnal. The first thing I did every day was open that hymnal. I slowly worked through it, singing a few hymns every day I must say, those sweet times of worship were so healing for me spiritually. During those months after my miscarriage the Lord opened His Word up to me and drew me to Him. I learned some important lessons about forgiveness, about the importance of worship, and many other life-changing truths. Wow! What a refreshing time it was to be back—hearing from the Lord, walking with Him, spending time with Him every day.

Those times were not always quiet and uninterrupted. Those times were almost always checkered with children asking questions, visitors coming through the house, or conversations I could hear going on outside. Cambodian culture does not afford much private time, so I had to block everyone out. Previously I saw this kind of time with God as inferior. I didn't want to sit down for any study or prayer without the perfect conditions. However, I finally reckoned with the fact that we lived in a culture where houseguests were the norm. Also, as the mother of three (and now five), I knew there was probably not going to be an ideal time for me to spend time with God. Yet if it were a priority, I would just have to make do, and so, by God's grace, I did.

During these years when our children are young and the needs and demands of ministry are so great, we desperately need daily time with God. Time with Him daily is an absolute must. Only when we're walking with God are we able to love each other selflessly. Only when we're walking with God will we be able to move past ourselves to meet the needs of others around us in His name.

TEND TO YOUR MARRIAGE BY UNDERSTANDING AND PURSUING GOD'S PURPOSES TOGETHER

A good and loving marriage is not an end to itself. Many marriage seminars and marriage-help books drop the ball here and fail to help focus couples on why God created marriage and the family. A good and loving marriage was created by God as a wonderful, beautiful, and satisfying means to a much greater end, to be a divine picture and a tool toward the pursuit of the eternal purposes of God. First, marriage was created as an earthly picture of the relationship God desires between Himself and His church, the body of Christ. Every groom and bride are to be models of the kind of love relationship that Christ redeemed every believer to enjoy with Himself. Second, every groom and bride have been joined together in order to serve His purposes on this earth.

A good and loving marriage can be a wonderful source of human happiness, and God is pleased in this. A marriage relationship will only begin to experience fully that happiness when a couple seeks to use their marriage as a picture to their children and others of what Christ desires with us and as a tool to worship Him, love others, bring others to faith in Christ, immerse them into the family of God, and help them to mature in His Word and Christlikeness.

When we first married, we must admit that we thought we were the happiest couple we knew. We still feel this way. We loved being together, no matter if it was having dinner alone, with others, at church, or doing chores around the house. Something that both of us began to experience secretly was that we found ourselves looking forward to time with each other far more than we looked forward to time with God, enjoying His fellowship. We began to enjoy and worship the creature more than the Creator, the gift more than the giver. Both of us felt it deep down, but we never said a word about it to each other. We did not want to admit that it was true, and besides it was all so wonderful.

Slowly our relationship and love for each other became the most important thing in our lives. Friendships were neglected. Extended family was neglected. Real and meaningful outreach efforts to lost neighbors and friends around us became almost nonexistent. The joy and eagerness we both once had to spend time alone with God, in His Word, and in communion with Him in prayer had all faded, although we would never let these things completely fall off. Our worship no longer had any passion. Life had spiraled down to being simply about us.

One day, several years after being married, we began to open up with each other about this issue, and the tears began to flow. We were so broken about how inward and selfish and empty our marriage had become. We still loved each other dearly, but there was no purpose in our marriage that truly honored God, and we knew it. The sad fact was that we were missionaries in Cambodia, called by God to bring His life and love to millions of desperate and searching people all around us. Yet we were missing out on what God wanted to do. So that afternoon we sat there in our home in Siem Reap, Cambodia, and asked God to forgive us.

Then we asked each other for forgiveness, and we started again. We began to examine His Word together and ask ourselves, "What are His eternal purposes for our marriage and family? How can they be defined? What do we need to start doing in our marriage and family to give all our energies and prayers in pursuit of these eternal purposes?" We came up with five eternal purposes, derived from the words of Christ Himself in two passages found in the Book of Matthew. The two passages are Matthew 22:37–40 and Matthew 28:19–20, also known as the great commandments and the Great Commission.

And He said to him, "'YOU SHALL LOVE THE LORD YOUR GOD WITH ALL YOUR HEART, AND WITH ALL YOUR SOUL, AND

WITH ALL YOUR MIND.' This is the great and foremost commandment. The second is like it, 'YOU SHALL LOVE YOUR
NEIGHBOR AS YOURSELF.' On these two commandments
depend the whole Law and the Prophets" (Matt. 22:37–40
NASB).

Go therefore and make disciples of all the nations, bap-
tizing them in the name of the Father and the Son and the
Holy Spirit, teaching them to observe all that I commanded
you; and lo, I am with you always, even to the end of the
age (Matt. 28:19–20 NASB).

We believe that everything Christ created us for and brought us
together to accomplish can be summed up in these two passages of
Scripture, expressed in five purposes. We believe they apply to us as
individuals in our personal walk with God and as a couple in our one-
flesh ministry together.

As individuals:

1. Know and love God.
2. Love and serve people.
3. Spread and reproduce His faith in others.
4. Become immersed in and cherish His family.
5. Obey and model His commands.

In ministry together:

1. Love and worship God.
2. Love and serve people.
3. Lead others to Him.
4. Immerse them in His family.
5. Teach them to obey whatever He commands.

Refocusing our lives and marriage around these eternal purposes
has given us a clear vision for our marriage and has slowly transformed
and energized our marriage and our family. It is difficult now to

imagine how we missed this important truth in our marriage, especially after seeing God work in such amazing and miraculous ways to bring us together and lead us toward marriage in the first place.

Looking back, it really was miraculous how the Lord brought us together. In fact, we love telling people the story, including how He brought both of us back to the United States after we had each lived overseas for a time, both arriving in the U.S. on the same day; how He lead me to call Amy's father, whom I had never met, to ask his advice about the direction of my life and ministry; how the Lord prompted me to ask Amy about her interests in missions on our first date, which was a significant issue in Amy's heart for a future husband; how He prompted me to talk to Amy about a special passage of Scripture God had used to speak to me on my birthday, which, I discovered months later, happened to be the verse God had given her for her future mate; and how I decided one morning that it was time to ask Amy's father for permission to propose marriage to her, only to find out that her father and mother had asked God for a sign that morning, that if I was God's choice for Amy I would come asking for her hand in marriage that very day. With all that God did to bring us together, it seems now that it should have been obvious to us that He was joining us together for purposes larger and much higher than ourselves.

The wonderful lesson we're learning is this: Life is not about us; it is about God and His eternal purposes. We can clearly see it now, and it's become the driving passion of our lives. Marriage is becoming an exciting adventure as we see it as a means to a greater divine purpose. Tending our marriage involves focusing our marriage on the purposes of God, and working to stay in step with Him to accomplish those purposes, looking to see what wonderful ways He will intervene to make it happen!

Tending your marriage is hard work at times, just like tending a garden. However, the harvest is worth more than most couples could imagine.

CHAPTER ELEVEN

Consumed, but with Whom?

Dear Dad and Mom,

As we were looking through a handful of pictures today, we found ourselves reliving many of the moments that were captured on film — moments in history that could have only been created in the crucible of life, moments that have left indelible marks in our character. From the hours and hours of sitting on the front porch swing to the many dates planned, memories fresh in our minds still make those moments seem like they just took place. With every snapshot feelings of joy, excitement, anxiety, and yes, even sorrow flooded our hearts. We couldn't help but acknowledge the vital role that you both played throughout our dating experience. For every occasion where sacrifice was displayed, counsel given, and love made known, we want to say "thank you!" Your delight in every detail of our lives has shown us a small portion of the Father's heart!

Dad and Mom, during the times where discipline was necessary for our good, thank you for maintaining your obedience to Scripture. We realize only in hindsight that it was an extension of your

*unconditional love. We can only imagine how difficult it was for you to
say, "You no longer have our blessing upon your relationship." The
sorrow that followed was truly the kind that produced a repentance
without any regrets! We thought we would never make it past that day,
and yet the Lord was gracious and kind. We will forever be grateful for
those words that shot past our blind love and caused us to realize our
misplaced priorities. Those words helped us understand that as individuals accountable to a living God, we must seek His blessing and His
favor before we can ever earn yours.*

*Thank you Dad and Mom for placing the counsel of the Lord before
your own, for remaining faithful to deliver the truth of God's Word,
and for the sensitivity to know when and how to give us your blessing.
With all of our hearts,*
Greg and Sarah

THE PORTRAIT OF A "MANN"

The desire to become a godly man dissipates when the object of your
affection is anything other than Christ. I don't believe anyone wakes
up one morning and decides to discontinue his pursuit of godliness.
As a matter of fact, nothing could be further from the truth regarding my life. Having been raised in a Christian home, the struggle to
assume my own identity in Christ ensued.

It wasn't until the age of thirteen that I finally realized the con-
cept of salvation as a free gift. Eternal life was not granted to those
who simply grew up in church, nor was it something they worked for,
nor was it something they received via their parents, but it was by
God's grace through faith. I was determined to live a life right before
others as a result of God's love shown to me. That same mentality
remained with me as I entered into a relationship with Sarah Jane
Elliff.

Keeping our relationship above reproach was at the top of my
list. To remain a man of integrity was my goal. At times even my own

convictions regarding our relationship confused me. Why should I stand outside Sarah's apartment at college when other guys walked in and out at their own free will visiting her roommates? The answer was clear; I wanted to guard my own heart. Why didn't we ever go into a room by ourselves; didn't we deserve some privacy as a couple? Perhaps, but not at the expense of our reputations.

We believed that "a good name is rather to be chosen than great riches, and loving favour rather than silver and gold" (Prov. 22:1). We heeded the command to flee every appearance of evil. Though outwardly we appeared to be living godly lifestyles, inwardly our hearts began to be led astray by the object we most desired, each other.

If you asked me during this time if everything was all right concerning my relationship with Sarah, my answer would have been a resounding yes! There was only one problem with that answer; it simply wasn't true. It certainly was in my eyes, yet it had become apparent to everyone around us that things weren't the same. Those closest to us began shooting up warning flares signaling our impending downfall, yet we mistook them for fireworks.

Being consumed with someone you love prior to marriage seems like an honest mistake, but it's a costly one. For Sarah and me, the warning signs were in full bloom. Every friend we had made up until this point somehow got shoved aside. Through the awesome power of neglect, we had burned every bridge that got us to this point. Though we never spent late or lonely hours together, we never went long without seeing each other. We were with each other constantly. If we went to a church fellowship, we made a beeline to each other. Others would have been lucky to make eye contact with us.

The old adage "familiarity breeds contempt" proved true. Long experience of someone or something can make one so aware of the faults that it causes them to regard the other as common. When our siblings or parents pointed out truth to us, we would become defensive as opposed to accepting criticism. Proverbs 28:1 described us perfectly, "The wicked flee when no one pursues" (NKJV). Things weren't all right; I was simply good at justifying.

About 6:30 p.m. on a Thursday afternoon I pulled up to the Elliff house at the invitaton of Bro. Tom himself. I had just left work and was anticipating this engagement for some time. The conversation that followed left me drowning in my own tears. Sitting on the front porch, Bro. Tom simply stated that as a father responsible for the upbringing of his daughter, he could no longer give his blessing on our relationship. The future just looked too dark—one that was slowly leaving Christ out of the picture. In my tears I stated that I no longer wanted to live, but rather I wanted to die! I was consumed. A statement all too removed from the apostle Paul who said, "For to me to live is Christ, and to die is gain" (Phil. 1:21). I left that evening not knowing what would happen next. All I knew was that something had to change.

Sarah and I made a pledge to each other that we would not resume dating until we once again had the blessing of her father. Little did we know it would span a period of six months—a relatively short period of time in your mind, a lifetime in ours.

Three and a half months of that time I spent in Zimbabwe, Africa, as a short-term missionary with the International Mission Board. My motivation for going was far removed from the compassionate heart that normally goes. I was trying to escape my problems, not fulfill the Great Commission. But as any missionary, I did have certain responsibilities that I had to accomplish on the trip. Foremost of which was the task of "rightly dividing the word of truth" (2 Tim. 2:15) to nationals. I found myself ill equipped.

Circumstances forced me once again to pick up the Word of God and handle it for myself. Hebrews 4:12 speaks of what happened in my life: "For the word of God is living and active and sharper than any two-edged sword, and piercing as far as the division of soul and spirit, of both joints and marrow, and able to judge the thoughts and intentions of the heart" (NASB). And judge it did. In Gweru, Zimbabwe, I recognized just how far I had removed myself from God—not geographically but spiritually. I had lost my first love. Brokenness and humility ushered me back to the States, where an earthly father awaited with his blessing.

THE PORTRAIT OF A WOMAN

Following a Sunday evening service, Dad asked if he could escort me (Sarah) back to the university I attended. Something in his voice indicated to me that a long serious talk awaited me in the car. It wasn't long before he began to share his heart with me. We began to talk about my relationship with Greg. I expected to receive some wise counsel, but I was unprepared for the disappointment of a father's broken heart. Perhaps it was the false hope located in the back of my mind that everything was going to be OK. Love truly is blind, isn't it?

My dad continued with sadness stretched across his face, "Sarah, I can no longer give you my blessing if you continue to date Greg." Silence followed. I was stunned. The words kept echoing in my mind with the hopes that I had misunderstood him. Though tears welled up in my eyes, I refrained from crying. My father, like any loving father, made sure that I was OK as I walked toward my dorm room, and I, like anyone else, pretended to be just that.

The Bible that I read many times before never seemed more important. With emotions too hard to bear alone, I grabbed it off my bed and sprinted toward the prayer room located in the freshmen dorm. With not a tear dropping yet, the door closed behind me, and sincerity burst forth. Never have I found myself more alone than I did that night, and never have I cried harder. I was so hurt, so frustrated. Loneliness found its place in my heart. Prior to this night I had made no effort to continue the relationships I once held so dear—relationships with friends as well as with God. Now, within a short period of time, my only friend would be taken away from me.

The thought of disobeying my father and continuing a relationship with Greg was only a fleeting thought. Engrained in my mind and proved throughout my life was the knowledge that my father loved me and knew what was best for me. One night would not change what was shown throughout a lifetime. It was consistent. With nothing else left for me to cling to, I opened God's Word and prayed with more intensity than I ever had before. The determination not to leave until I found God's presence and peace remained with me until the early hours of the morning.

With the hope of a new day before me, I crouched down in the inner recesses (dirty clothes pile) of my dorm closet so my roommates wouldn't hear me and called Greg. From there, he and I began to express our sorrow through the lens of tears—not so much for what we had done as for what we had become. We began that day a journey that lasted six months—six months of learning to fall in love with Jesus all over again.

LESSONS LEARNED FROM LOVERS

Job 23:10 says, "He knows the way I take; when He has tried me, I shall come forth as gold" (NASB). God is concerned about both the process and the product. James 1:4 echoes that by pleading with us to "let patience have her perfect work, that ye may be perfect and entire, wanting nothing," following the trials in our lives. It's the result as well as the race. Without a doubt though, the process or race can be some of the most painful days, especially when human emotion is involved. My father-in-law says that the principles of God's Word are like the grain of the universe. Going with the grain makes for a smooth ride, but if you go against the grain, you'll wind up with splinters. Here are some of the principles, or lessons, we learned through the process.

1. Love truly is blind; when you fail to see your own faults, listen to what others are saying.
    It seems like yesterday that one of my sisters approached me (Greg) out of concern. Having a bird's-eye view of my relationship with Sarah gave her the advantage. I was blinded, smitten with the love of a sophomore in college. "Greg, how come you never hang out with your friends anymore?" What? That was news to me. I spent plenty of time with them in the classroom. Statements of justification became commonplace as the counsel others offered was either ignored or rejected.
    Go to any restaurant in the world, remain there long enough, and eventually you'll find a lover lost in the gaze of another. It's as if no one else exists but the two of them. It doesn't just stop at the end of a good meal. Feelings of tender affection for another seem to pursue you with every step you take, and so does your seeing impairment. In

The Merchant of Venice, William Shakespeare wrote, "Lovers cannot see the pretty follies that themselves commit." Only in the context of love do we find ourselves oblivious to the obvious. What appears to be a healthy relationship in our eyes turns out to be a relationship that is suffering before all.

When you fail to see your own faults, listen to what others are saying. The proverbial wisdom that is offered by Solomon serves to instruct us in this matter. "Hear, my son, your father's instruction and do not forsake your mother's teaching; indeed, they are a graceful wreath to your head, and ornaments about your neck" (Prov. 1:8–9 NASB). Not only do your parents serve as counselors but your friends do as well. "Oil and perfume make the heart glad, so a man's counsel is sweet to his friend" (Prov. 27:9 NASB). "Iron sharpens iron, so one man sharpens another" (Prov. 27:17 NASB). To ignore the counsel of God, parents, and friends is to invite unnecessary feelings of pain, resentment, and sorrow to your heart (see also Prov. 1:24–33; 2:1–5; 3:1; 4:1–5, 10, 20–22; 5:1, 7, 13; 6:20–22; 7:1–2, 24; 8:32–34; 9:9; 10:17; 11:14; 13:1, 14; 14:5; 15:5, 22, 32; 17:10; 19:20; 24:6; 25:11–14; 27:5–6, 17; 28:23).

2. Never place yourself in a position relationally that you can't fulfill realistically.

Emotion has been defined as "a mental state that arises spontaneously rather than through conscious effort." It took no effort on my part to become emotionally attached to Sarah. It was something that happened naturally as our friendship progressed. God does not expect us to separate our humanity from living, nor does He want us to abandon our emotions. It's impossible. However, He does expect us to exhibit self-control in every area of our lives, including the emotional aspect. Proverbs says that a person without self-control is as defenseless as a city with broken-down walls (25:28). I yielded to the temptation to say that Sarah was mine. I gave in but not without reaping the consequences, for jealousy was soon to follow. The truth was evident. I was not in a position to say that I am my beloved's, and she is mine (Song of Sol. 2:16). If that were the case, we would have been married. I placed myself in an emotional position that I wasn't prepared to back up.

Whether physical, emotional, financial, or spiritual, human tendency is to place yourself in a position relationally that promises much but delivers little. It's like massive rain clouds that cover the sky yet produce nothing. For some this may mean little, but for the farmer whose life depends on the rain falling to the ground and watering his crops, it means everything! Not only do the clouds produce a false hope, but they also produce a sick heart, one that's filled with disappointment.

The same is true for the one who places the relational cart before the horse. Solomon tells us that "hope deferred makes the heart sick, but desire fulfilled is a tree of life" (Prov. 13:12 NASB). Nothing happens when the horse is behind the cart, nor does it when one promises marriage to the woman he loves but has no sense of vocational direction for his life. On the other hand, when the man who is financially stable pledges his love to a woman (provided that every other area of his life is stable as well), he places himself in a position for something real to take place. The desire to move forward in their relationship has now become a potential reality, not just a false hope.

3. Seek the Father's blessing on your relationship, and you'll no doubt find a father's blessing.

Following an evening worship service, I found myself racing out of the auditorium to catch my future father-in-law heading for his office. With a wrenched stomach, I finally worked up the nerve to ask him a question. Through stammering teeth, I asked if his daughter could get a drink with me at the local fast-food chain. His fast-paced walk came to a complete standstill, and with peering eyes and a blank expression on his face, he asked, "Is she thirsty?" The pause that followed made me believe he really wanted an answer. Thankfully, he broke the silence with a little humor. From that moment on, I realized the power of a blessing.

Sarah and I made it a matter of practice to ask her father's permission to date. But somewhere along the way his blessing became more important to me than the Heavenly Father's blessing. What I didn't understand was that the two were interrelated. The more I placed Sarah above Christ, the less I had God's blessing; and the less I had God's blessing, the less I had her father's blessing. It was a vicious cycle that could only be broken by a return to the Father.

In *The Gift of the Blessing,* Gary Smalley mentions several basic elements of the blessing in the Old Testament, of which one is relevant. Used more than 640 times in the Old Testament alone, a blessing pictured a special future for the person being blessed, as was in the case of Isaac and Jacob (see Gen. 27:28–29). What is ironic is that without God's blessing I did not have her father's blessing, and without her father's blessing I had no future with Sarah. The equation was simple: Without God's blessing I had nothing special to look forward to. However, if that were true, then the opposite must be true as well: With God's blessing I had an incredible future awaiting me.

During our six-month separation my Heavenly Father spoke to me through His Word. Ecclesiastes 7:18 says, "It is good that you grasp one thing and also not let go of the other, for the one who fears God comes forth with both of them" (NASB). It was as if God was telling me to cling to everything that pertains to Him and His ways and to rest my hand gently on everything that pertains to Sarah. Then and only then would I come forth with both.

Coming to a point of submission to God's will was not easy, even though it was what I wanted. Through the fires of separation, I realized my need for brokenness. If I was to learn anything from this experience, it was going to come through this painful channel.

But like any great man or woman of faith, you must first endure the storm to enjoy the rainbow. The rains of sorrow and despair fell pretty hard during our separation, but showers of blessing were soon to follow. I arrived back from Zimbabwe with a heart that sought the blessing of my Heavenly Father and to a lover who wanted the same. Before long I found myself sitting on the same front porch where I had been denied the blessing of an earthly father, only this time, I received one. If we seek the *Father's* blessing on our relationships first, we will no doubt find a *father's* blessing.

4. The characteristics that you long for in a spouse must first be present in you.

I can remember as a high school student being challenged by my student minister to write a list of qualities I wanted in a spouse. I had not given it much thought until that point, but I decided to oblige him and write them down. I never dreamed that by the age of twenty-two, that list would become obsolete, but it did. God sent me a young lady who was the totality of every good and pleasing thought I ever had.

Your life should be the consummation of every characteristic you desire in your future mate. Tim Jones, a friend of mine, once shared with me a quote that I've become fond of through the years. Simply stated, it says, "Kings marry queens!" In other words, what you long for in a spouse someday must first be present in you. If you desire her to be beautiful, then what are you doing to make yourself more attractive? If you want her to be spiritually sensitive to the Lord, then how are you attuning your ear to the voice of the Lord?

Too often we have such high expectations for a mate. Though high standards are good, you're only setting yourself up for self-defeat. Why would anyone be attracted to an individual who doesn't live up to the expectations he establishes for others? I can assure you though, lowering your standards would not be the right thing to do; seeing them come to fruition in your own life would.

5. *The desire to become a husband must be preceded by the desire to become a bride.*

As I sat alone in the living room of an African pastor's house in Zimbabwe, Africa, I found myself longing to be wed to Sarah. Many nights had been spent with this thought rolling around in my head. Not only were we separated geographically with thousands of miles between us, but we were separated relationally because we lacked four simple words from her father, "You have my blessing!" God had to take me to the ends of the earth to help me understand that I was His bride and that it wasn't just at the point of salvation that I assumed that position but every day that followed.

Marriage doesn't stop at the altar; it begins there. We say we want to "get married" as if marriage is a definitive point in time. The ceremony is; marriage is not! The same is true spiritually. Becoming a bride of Christ begins with salvation, but it does not end there. Christ wants us to recognize that our marriage to him is not an emotional ceremony where we say, "I do" but a lifetime of saying, "I will!"

I was born again seven years prior to this moment and was living as a spiritual adulterer in the eyes of God. My desire was not to live as the bride of Christ each and every day of my life but to live as the husband of Sarah. May your desire to become the bride of Christ always precede your desire of becoming a husband. (For references regarding the church as the bride of Christ, see Isa. 62:5; 2 Cor. 11:2; Rev. 19:7; 21:2; 22:17.)

The question isn't whether you are consumed, but with whom are you consumed? We are charged to love the Lord our God with all of our hearts, and with all of our souls, and with all of our minds (Deut. 6:5; Matt. 22:37; Mark 12:30). Our passion for God should run so deep that it consumes every aspect of our lives. For the moment you take one step away from God, you end up taking two steps away from the lover you desire. "Delight yourself in the LORD, and He will give you the desires of your heart" (Ps. 37:4 NASB).

CHAPTER TWELVE

Trying Times

Dear Dad and Mom,

As you all know, we have had such an emotional and spiritual struggle these last several years trying to conceive our first child. We were so thrilled several months ago to tell you the new work God had wrought in Becky's womb. Thank you so much for imparting to us such an appreciation and desire for children and then for celebrating with us this child's conception.

However, with tremendous grief we must tell you that our baby has died. After hours of torture in the emergency room last night with no conclusion and with a horrifying ultrasound this morning, we discovered that our baby died about four weeks ago.

Nothing in our lives has ever prepared us for such a devastating loss. Years of frustration over our infertility seemed finally to be resolved in this little one. Now it seems as if we are the brunt of some divine prank.

These horrible events are taking a toll on us and our marriage. We don't know if we should blame God, blame each other, or blame ourselves.

It seems that every problem, every bad day, and every argument boil down to this one great frustration.

We know you, also, are deeply saddened by the loss of this child. Today we ask that you pray for us. Pray for our relationship to God, and pray for our marriage.

These are trying times,

Jon and Becky Elliff

Today's society portrays children as a burden both financially and physically. Children are seen as a hindrance to the "more important" things in life. They will make you poor and keep you from doing the things that you want to do. This view of children, however, never crossed our minds going into marriage. We were so fortunate to grow up in a wonderful church where children are considered to be a special blessing from the Lord. The biblical view of children has been embraced by most, if not all, of the members at First Southern. Many families have five or more children. We came to the marriage altar with hopes and dreams of starting our own family soon after the wedding.

Even before we married, we decided that we would not use any sort of birth control. We believed that God was sovereign over all life, and we would conceive in His timing, not our own. We had also discovered that no birth control pill had ever been proven 100 percent nonabortive, and that is a risk we would never want to take.

We had not prepared ourselves for what lay ahead of us. We thought surely God would honor our decision to trust Him, and He would give us a child within a few months. After a few months passed by, we continued trusting Him. After a year went by with no child, we continued trusting Him. It seemed to us that God was withholding a blessing from us. When the time continued to pass without any signs of pregnancy, we began to question why God was not choosing to bless us with the precious gift of a child.

We began to struggle through this difficult time of waiting and waiting. We wondered if there was sin in our lives that had gone unconfessed. We wondered if our marriage relationship was for some reason not worthy of receiving blessing. We wondered if we could do something to show God that we were ready and willing to raise godly children. After all, wasn't this one of the reasons for marriage? We soon realized that having a child, for us, would not be as easy as we thought. We realized that we were in this for the long haul, that we had to trust God in His sovereignty, and wait patiently for His hand to bless us with a child.

Exactly two years after we were married, we conceived our first child. What a joy it was to find out that after such a long time of waiting and wondering we would soon experience the blessing of giving life to our own child. We cried and thanked God for choosing to impart this blessing to us. We prayed for the health and well-being of our little one. We announced to all of our family and friends about the pregnancy. We felt so fortunate, and we just knew that God would surely preserve this little life that He created.

However, to our horror and disbelief, thirteen weeks into the pregnancy we found out that our little one had died at just nine weeks gestation. Now through tears of grief we had to announce to our friends and family that our baby had gone to be with the Lord. This was the most devastating time that we had ever faced, and we had to work through it together. Not only did we have to depend on each other; we had to depend so much more on the comfort that can come only from the Lord. This ushered us into a time of spiritual growth and also into a time of growing closer to each other.

We certainly have never assumed that our disappointment and tragedy is the worst thing that can happen to any couple. No doubt many readers have gone through tragic events of much greater proportion. However, through this tragic chain of events, we believe God issued a certain amount of grit and wisdom upon us that we can share with others. We had to deal with both frustration and despair. We countered these with biblical comfort and a keen sense of resolve.

DEALING WITH FRUSTRATION

The most common human emotion after a traumatic event is frustration. Frustration, anger, and blame are all normal human responses. When Adam and Eve sinned in the Garden of Eden, their initial response was blame. Our feelings after our loss included blaming God, being angry at each other, and being frustrated at ourselves. We were angry that our goals were blocked, and we were also a bit angry with God. We had to grapple with this emotion, and though we were confused, we wanted to do it in a way that still honored Him.

Evil is a problem in every marriage. Whether it is a natural evil, such as our tragedy, or a moral evil, as long as Satan is prince of this earth, evil will invade our marriages. As we looked evil square in the eye, we knew that this great heartbreak would prepare us for heartbreaks to come. The way we responded to infertility and then the death of our little child would help us face evil that might invade our marriage in the future.

We realized early on that we could not blame God. The typical presumption of a sovereign God is that He teases finite humanity with tragic events such as this. In response, people ask questions such as, "Why did you do this, God?" or, "Why didn't you prevent this, God?" These questions harken to the age-old problem of evil. How could a loving God do evil or at least allow evil to happen?

When evil invades a marriage, we must first resist the urge to blame God. The Bible clearly shows that God is incapable of committing any evil act. When we say, "God can do anything; He is omnipotent," what we are essentially saying is that God can do anything that is *logically* possible. Just as it is impossible for a cow to birth a canine, it is impossible for a holy God to commit sin. God declares that He is holy (Lev. 11:44–45), that He cannot be tempted to sin (James 1:13), and that the security of our salvation is based on the fact that it is "impossible for God to lie" (Heb. 6:18 NASB).

For finite, sinful humans to lift the finger of accusation and point it to a holy God is ludicrous. To do so would be blasphemy and would betray our limited faith that He is sovereign and works things out for our good and His glory. We can neither blame Him for the evil nor blame Him for not preventing the evil. As gratuitous as the evil may be, we do not have the mind of God and, until heaven, may never understand the reason God permitted Satan to attack our family. So before we even began to deal with the devastating miscarriage, we had to commit never to blame God.

Another commitment is to resist the urge to blame yourselves. This commitment is particularly challenging because the blame can so easily rest on one or the other of the partners. We went through times of feeling that our bodies were inadequate or not up to the task of childbearing. We soon realized that when we put the blame on ourselves or each other, our marriage relationship would suffer. We would begin to feel self-pity and dejection. This cannot be healthy for any marriage. When an evil such as this invades, Satan will tempt us to point fingers and guilt at our spouse or at ourselves.

Before a couple can make this commitment, they may need preparation. In 1 Corinthians 11:30, Paul scolds the Corinthians for the outright sin of the church, "For this reason many among you are weak and sick" (NASB). God evidently had allowed the Corinthians to suffer illness because of their sin.

Though Christians should not assume any kind of trouble is a direct punishment for a certain sin (see John 9:1–3), we should live in a manner of ready and regular repentance. We should be willing to search and test ourselves by confessing our sins, and striving for holiness (Matt. 5:8). God may have allowed evil to befall our marriage in order for us to expel some petty sin prevalent in our lives.

Hebrews 12:5–7 is helpful here:

> And you have forgotten the exhortation which is addressed to you as sons,
> "MY SON, DO NOT REGARD LIGHTLY THE DISCIPLINE OF THE LORD,
> NOR FAINT WHEN YOU ARE REPROVED BY HIM;
> FOR THOSE WHOM THE LORD LOVES HE DISCIPLINES,
> AND HE SCOURGES EVERY SON WHOM HE RECEIVES."
> It is for discipline that you endure; God deals with you as with sons; for what son is there whom his father does not discipline? (NASB).

The point the author of Hebrews is making is not that we ought to see every ache and pain as a divine spanking. The passage was written to use every such invasion of evil as a reminder to confess, to repent, and to develop the discipline and mettle required of us. God allowed these things in our lives not to harm or torture us but to make us better. So before we avoid false guilt, we must pray as the psalmist: "Search me, O God, and know my heart; try me and know my anxious thoughts; and see if there be any hurtful way in me, and lead me in the everlasting way" (Ps. 139:23–24 NASB). This cleansing process has helped us in our marriage as we have had to deal with the Lord's building discipline in our lives.

Ultimately, frustration and anger are the product of the desire to blame. In Revelation 12:10, Satan is called the "accuser of our brethren." When we are challenged with tragedy, we must commit not to blame God, our spouse, or ourselves. We must commit to making this a time of learning and spiritual development rather than blame and rage.

FACING DESPAIR

After we dealt with the temptation to blame, the next thing we faced was despair. Is there something physically wrong with us? Will we ever have children? Will we have another two years of frustration and disappointment? As these questions invaded our thoughts, we realized there was only one place to turn to relieve our grief and despair: the Word of God.

Who better than Jesus Christ to identify with our sorrow and grief? "He was despised and forsaken of men, a man of sorrows and acquainted with grief; And like one from whom men hide their face He was despised, and we did not esteem Him" (Isa. 53:3 NASB). When we look to Jesus, the author and finisher of our faith, we can know the next verse in Isaiah 53 is true, "Surely our griefs He Himself bore, and our sorrows He carried" (NASB).

We learned two truths concerning the Word of God that we believe are important in every marriage tragedy. First, we must be consumed with finding the comfort the Bible gives. Psalm 33:18–20 says, "Behold, the eye of the LORD is on those who fear Him, on those who hope for His lovingkindness, to deliver their soul from death and to keep them alive in famine. Our soul waits for the LORD. He is our help and our shield" (NASB). Nothing is more comforting than finding loving-kindness through the words of the tortured psalmist, the precaution of a passionate preacher *("Be anxious for nothing,"* Phil. 4:6 NASB), or the prayers of our loving Savior *("Keep them from the evil one,"* John 17:15 NASB).

We must also find a special passage on which we can frequently meditate to relieve our grief. We developed a list of passages that spoke to us individually and typed them out to display in our house. Whenever we found ourselves in the midst of grief, we could turn to those passages for comfort and hope. One passage that guided us through that time was Psalm 50:15, "Call upon Me in the day of trouble; I shall rescue you, and you will honor Me" (NASB). We have realized that just as we need guidance from specific passages in the Bible, we also need comfort. We realized that no book, personality, friend, or counselor could surpass the comforting words of the Scripture.

RESPONDING TO EACH OTHER

Though we grew closer to each other as God comforted us through His Word and as we learned of the fidelity He was developing in us, we still had much to learn about each other. Becky needed to learn some things about Jon, and Jon needed to learn some things about Becky.

The wife's response to her husband. Men and women deal with grief and frustration in different ways. Men tend to be less emotional, whereas women tend to be very emotional. If she is not careful, a wife can become bitter if she feels that her husband "gets over" a tragedy more quickly than she does. I had to cope with this issue for many days and nights.

Dealing with infertility and the miscarriage took a toll on me emotionally and spiritually. Each day was a struggle to be joyful about my situation—a situation the Lord had so tenderly placed on me. Every time I saw a mother with her children or an expectant mother, my heart would sink. It reminded me of the devastation and loss I had encountered in trying to become a mother myself. Many times I caught myself asking, "Why would God choose to bless *her* with a precious child and not *me?*" It was the most emotionally trying time in my life.

Yet looking at my husband, I couldn't tell he was struggling through anything like this. He was so even tempered. He could concentrate on and think about other things besides infertility and losing our first child. This hurt me badly. Many nights we toiled through discussing the differences in the way we grieved. There were times when I thought, *How could he already be over this?* And I'm sure he was thinking at the same time, *Why is she still struggling with this?*

The Lord commands wives through the words of Paul in Ephesians 5:22–24 to "be subject to your own husbands, as to the Lord. For the husband is the head of the wife, as Christ also is the head of the church, He Himself being the Savior of the body. But as the church is subject to Christ, so also the wives ought to be to their husbands in everything" (NASB). Does *everything* mean in grieving too, Lord? The answer was a resounding yes! I soon realized that in this time especially I needed to submit to my husband's authority and leadership.

I was soon aware that my husband *was* still dealing with pain and grief. The only difference between my grieving and his grieving was that he was doing it biblically. He was counting it all joy. He was allowing the comfort of the Lord to comfort him. He was fully trusting that God would provide us with children some day. He was not worried about the future of our family. When I began to follow Jon's leadership in this area, I was a much more joyful and pleasant person!

Jon was leading me to more faith in what the Lord had for our family. If I had never learned this all-important lesson of submission, I might still be moping around feeling sorry for myself. Yes, there are still days when I am saddened by the loss of our child. However, I cannot let the darkness of despair and depression rule my life or my family. As a wife, I must trust the Lord and His plan over my own fears and doubts. Through this terribly trying time, I am thankful that the Lord taught me this wonderful lesson of submitting myself to my husband and letting him be the spiritual leader and head in our home, just as Christ is the head of the church.

The husband's response to his wife. I had never been more devastated in my life than when we discovered our child had died. I thought I was holding out pretty well until the terrible-news-bearing ultrasound technician left the room. Raw emotion poured out as we wept together. Nevertheless, within several weeks, though I still grieved over our loss, I finally found respite from my visible emotions.

Becky, on the other hand, had a long way to go to find this relief. As I searched for my role next to my grieving and emotional wife, several thoughts crossed my mind: *I've figured out how to deal with this. I need to show her how she can do the same. She just needs to pour her heart out to me and let me determine how we can begin to heal. I am to be the spiritual leader of this household, and I must set the pattern as one who truly believes the promises of God in the Bible.* But this was new territory for me, and I had no idea what I was doing.

One familiar passage of Scripture, however, enlightened my understanding of what I was to do as the husband: Ephesians 5:28–29, "So husbands ought also to love their own wives as their own bodies. He who loves his own wife loves himself; for no one ever hated his own flesh, but nourishes and cherishes it, just as Christ also does the church" (NASB).

The first, and most obvious, application of this passage is that, as the husband of my wife, *I must nourish her and I must cherish her.* When Paul used the word "nourish," he was simply referring to feeding (cf. NIV, "he feeds it"). Food and drink are necessary stuff for living. A married man is required to provide the "necessary stuff" for his wife. For many men this comes easily. We revel in being the breadwinners for the family and work hard to provide for our wives.

While we are great at feeding ourselves, we are not so great at caring for our bodies. The word *cherish* is simply the word for *care.* It is where we get the word *therapy.* Most of us are in desperate need of physical care. Sadly, for many of us the parallel is true. We are great at providing for the family, working long hours, living in a comfortable house, giving wonderful gifts to our children; but as a rule, we are terrible at caring for our wives.

During times of great grief, God has placed us alongside our wives not only to nourish them but also to care for them. I realized quickly that I was to provide the emotional support, encouragement, special dates, gifts, and anything else she needed. In times like this I was not be her instructor, leader, or boss but her companion, support, and servant.

As I unveiled the truth in this Ephesians passage, I discovered something more vital than caring for Becky. The end of the verse says that He "nourishes and cherishes it, just as Christ also does the church" (NASB). After months of struggling to be the sole caregiver for my wife, I realized that ultimately Christ would comfort my wife. I could do my job, be her servant, do special things for her, but I had to trust that Christ had her in His hand.

As men our tendency is to want to be idolized by our wives. We want them to believe we are their all in all and their one source of inspiration. We want them to tell their friends with a breathy voice, "He's the wind beneath my wings." Isn't this what the secular world tells us true love is? The Bible says this drooling, disgusting infatuation is idolatry. Though God has called us as leaders to nourish and cherish our wives, we ultimately leave our partners in the hands of almighty God and in the arms of a caring Savior.

FINAL THOUGHTS

We have not sought in this chapter to be comprehensive in dealing with pain or frustration about infertility or miscarriage. What we have sought to do is to share how the Lord carried us through the most troubling time of our lives. In hindsight our marriage was strengthened during this devastating time. Through His loving mercy the Lord has brought us to a much more intimate relationship with Him and a much more intimate relationship with each other. Since these tragic events, God has continued to bless our marriage. Chloe Elizabeth was born September 2002. By grasping the greater plan of God, we committed not to blame God or each other, to face down despair with the Word, and to strengthen our marriage by living out the roles given to us in Ephesians 5.

PART THREE

Some Final Words for the Family

The Journey

In-laws

A Legacy of Faith

*W*e didn't want to let the opportunity pass without addressing some often overlooked issues in family life: the in-law issue; how wives and mothers can keep the "journey" in perspective; and finally, the importance of leaving a godly legacy for those who will follow.

We often tell people that family life is not a science but that it is an art. Good families are not the result of just pushing all the right buttons, attending the right seminars, or reading the right books. Good families begin with being attentive to your own walk with God and then to the important people who make up your family.

In this parting section we invite you to write your own letters to lovers. They're just waiting to read *your* mail.

CHAPTER THIRTEEN

The Journey

Dear Beth, Amy, Sarah, and Becky,

Seeing you walk through the various stages of life is so thrilling. Watching you grow up and marry God's man for you has been a blessed gift from the Lord to me.

Thanksgiving 1999 was a memorable time for me. We were gathered at your house, Beth, since Dad and I were in transition after the house fire (February 1999) and the tornado which hit our condominium (May 1999). As the ten of us were gathered around the table, we were sharing God's blessings in the previous year.

I remembered the years before. Your dad had given me a necklace with six golden beads to symbolize the journey together that the six of us (Dad, me, and our four children, Beth Amy, Sarah, and Jon) were taking. In 1988, when Beth became Tony's princess bride, I added another golden bead. In January 1995, at the wedding of David and Amy's dreams, I had one more bead on my necklace. In 1997 Sarah married her childhood sweetheart, Greg. As I added a gold bead for Greg, I wondered when and who Jon would marry.

What sheer joy and delight it was for Jon to choose a girl we'd known, admired, and loved for years, Greg's younger sister, Becky. As we sat around the table, I saw the circle and my necklace were complete.

As you know I still wear that necklace. Often, I use it to remind me to pray for each of you as you pass through the events in your lives. Life is a journey. As I've traveled on this journey, a Scripture passage has meant a lot to me. I would like to share with you five things from Psalm 84:5–7 that have helped me along the way.

Perhaps these truths will help you on your journey.

Love,

Mom

This summer our family will travel from our different homes to a house in Colorado, which we have rented for all twenty-eight of us. The paths of each of our trips will be somewhat different, and the baggage we each take along will be designed to meet our family's needs. Yet we all have one goal: some long awaited days of memory making.

My life has been a journey with many joys, some heartaches, and a few unanswered questions along the way. Years ago I was struggling with an upcoming adjustment I was going to have to make. A precious older friend encouraged me with a few verses from the Psalms. As I have studied this Scripture many times over the years, I've discovered five things that have made my journey much smoother.

"Blessed is the man whose strength is in You, whose heart is set on pilgrimage. As they pass through the Valley of Baca, They make it a spring; The rain also covers it with pools. They go from strength to strength; Each one appears before God in Zion" (Ps. 84:5–7 NKJV).

STRENGTH IS FOUND ONLY IN THE LORD

"Blessed is the man whose strength is in You." The Scripture implies there is strength in other places, but if one wants to be blessed, he must find his strength in the Lord. This truth is contrary to what the world teaches. Even an old favorite children's book, *The Little Engine that Could*, reinforces the mantra, "You've got it within yourself to do anything you want." Of course, to some degree, this worldly wisdom is true. The flesh can be trained. Yet anyone who has lived even a few years realizes there comes a point of recognizing your weakness. Naturally, the first step for a believer is recognizing he cannot save himself. It's only Jesus.

Philippians 4:13, "I can do all things through Christ who strengthens me" (NKJV), is a familiar verse that needs to be considered seriously. Christ's strength saves us, and Christ's strength accomplishes all things that will be blessed.

The year 1982 found me seated beside our fourteen-year-old daughter, Beth, in the hospital in Harare, Zimbabwe. Our car had been sabotaged, resulting in an accident that left Beth with multiple broken bones and third-degree burns.

I have never done well in hospitals. The smells, the sights, and the sounds had several times added up to embarrassing episodes of me being on the floor, people fanning me, or using smelling salts to bring me around. I knew I had to keep my wits about me to help care for Beth, but it just wasn't in me. That's when I trusted completely in the Lord's strength. The nearly six weeks of confinement to the burn ward with Beth was a tremendous victory and a truly great lesson of relying on the Lord.

Trusting in God's strength alone is sometimes easier for big crises. I have to remind myself to trust Him every day for strength. I want to be blessed, don't you? The only way to experience the blessing God has for me is to live a life of faith. God is pleased when we simply take Him at His Word.

LIFE IS A PILGRIMAGE

When we let the Lord be our strength, we will be blessed. The next phrase says, that his "heart is set on pilgrimage." Where is this pilgrimage leading us? The last phrase in verse 7 tells us it's before God in Zion! That's where this journey on earth is leading us!

This life is not the ultimate. It is a pilgrimage *to* the ultimate for the follower of Christ. I can't think of a woman in Scripture who is a better illustration of a heart set on pilgrimage than Ruth. First, though from a pagan culture, she married into a family who believed in the one true God. Not too far into her marriage, her young husband died. Having turned her back on her family's pagan culture, she chose to follow her mother-in-law back to her family home, where Ruth had never been. The following days brought incredibly hard work, marriage to a kinsman, and then a family. Throughout the story we never hear Ruth complain of the incredible changes that came into her life. She had her heart set on pilgrimage.

I have watched with joy as our children, David and Amy Jarboe, sold their dream home and many of their possessions, moved to a foreign country, settled for a while to learn the language, then moved again to a house for a few years to do their work, came home for stateside assignment, only to return to Cambodia for another term. All of this was done not without tears but with an acceptance of the pilgrimage the Lord had for them and their five children.

As Tom and I and our four children got ready to go to the last service in the church Tom had pastored for nine years, I had a lump in my throat. We dearly loved that church in Tulsa, Oklahoma. As the service closed, we stood and sang a favorite chorus, "Our God Reigns." As we sang, I wept, wondering how we could leave this church where the presence of God was so real!

Yet God had told us specifically that Zimbabwe was the next stop on our pilgrimage. Several months later our family landed in the Republic of South Africa to purchase a car to drive north to Zimbabwe. We were there over the weekend and went to an English language church on Sunday morning. As I took a bulletin from an usher, I glanced at the planned service. There listed among the songs was the chorus, "Our God Reigns." I felt my eyes fill with tears and asked "Lord, what are You trying to tell me?"

The next day we began our journey to Zimbabwe. The ensuing weeks found us settling into our new home and loving the beautiful people and land of Zimbabwe. Because of the war, there was a curfew in Zimbabwe, so we didn't get out much in the evenings. However, we decided to venture out one Sunday evening to an English language church, close to our house. The weather was warm, and it was a lovely evening. As we walked up to the church, with its windows and doors propped open, we realized the service had already started. As we entered the building, the dear believers were singing, "Our God Reigns!" I joined in singing realizing, finally, that God reigns in my home church; He reigns in all the world; He reigns all along this pilgrimage of mine! That's how I know I can make it on this pilgrimage. He's with me.

YOUR WEEPING CAN BECOME REJOICING

How can weeping become rejoicing? Looking at Psalm 84:6, we see one passing through the Valley of Baca (Weeping). In that valley two things happen. First, they make it a spring, and second, rain also covers it with pools. So here I am, trusting only in the Lord's strength, realizing my life here on earth is just a pilgrimage to the Lord, but now I come to a time of weeping in my life. What is my response to be?

I cannot actually make a spring, but I do know that springs are hidden underground. So as I look for the hidden water in my valley, the Lord sends rains until I am overflowing with pools of water! I know "that all things work together for good to those who love God, to those who are the called according to His purpose" (Rom. 8:28 NKJV). As I make my way through this valley of weeping, I end up joyful for I see the big picture of what God has for my life.

When our son, Jon, was taking drivers education (age fifteen), he felt compelled to come home and teach me (age forty-five) how to drive. He said, "Mom, you just need to get the big picture to make it safely down the road." This is good advice for drivers and for one who wants to navigate safely through life. Of course Jon also told me *I needed* a turbocharged car instead of our gray slow-moving family van.

Mary Magdalene was weeping at the cross (Mark 15:40) when Jesus died. Did she see the big picture? If she did, she was among the few. Three days later when Jesus appeared first to her (Mark 16:9), it all became clear. Jesus had explained everything, but sometimes it takes a little time to understand all he's doing.

The scars our daughter, Beth, received in the car accident in Zimbabwe have been a constant reminder of God's protection and provision for her. Beth's own children understand how God brought her through a time of weeping to a place of real joy.

BUILD ON PAST VICTORIES

"They go from strength to strength" is a challenging phrase. When toddlers take their first steps, they get the first taste of the victory of walking, and they want more. When the Lord gives us a victory, we can go on trusting Him for more. Another benefit we as believers have is that lessons learned in the past can continue to help us.

"For whatever things were written before were written for our learning, that we through the patience and comfort of the Scriptures might have hope" (Rom. 15:4 NKJV). The Book of Deuteronomy could be called the Book of Remembrances. The new generation of the children of Israel stood on the brink of the promised land, and one more time God's chosen leader reminded them of past victories to encourage them to press on.

Remember how God rescued and redeemed you when you couldn't do it for yourself? The same is true of our lives. We must remember the victories God has given us and lean into Him to bring us through again.

Our two youngest children, Sarah and Jon, married a brother and sister. Greg Mann and his sister, Becky Mann Elliff, come from a family in which they have witnessed over and over the victories of two incredible parents. The Mann's fifth child, Rachel, had difficulties at birth and as a result has a severe case of cerebral palsy. Because of the attitude and testimony of their parents, the other Mann children learned to go from strength to strength.

Then came a testing time for our sweet daughter-in-law Becky. After much prayer and waiting, Becky and Jon were blessed with a child. I took Becky shopping, where she saw an adorable red romper and sweater. I promised to get it for Becky if she had a girl. The next week Becky had a miscarriage. We all grieved. Our daughter Beth was especially heartbroken, for her own daughter was due in two months. As soon as Beth's baby girl was born, a package came in the mail from Aunt Becky. The adorable red romper we'd seen was carefully wrapped for Beth's baby girl. Becky had seen her mother and dad be joyful for others when their hearts were broken. Becky was going from strength to strength.

Perhaps you don't come from a family that has been an example to you. Then you must use the Scriptures as your model, trusting Jesus all the way to carry you from strength to strength. You will be a model for those who follow you.

YOU'LL ONE DAY STAND BEFORE JESUS

This one truth, if remembered on a consistent basis, will motivate you to follow all the previous truths. Why do I need to get any strength I possess from the Lord? All my righteous deeds are like filthy rags, and I want to have righteous deeds to present to Jesus when I see Him.

Why did I need to remember that life is a pilgrimage? When I enter the presence of Jesus, I will see this life as it really is, a pilgrimage into His eternal presence. Why must I realize my weeping will become rejoicing? Then I'll understand it all and see it face-to-face. Then all my tears will be wiped away.

Why must I go from strength to strength? So that when I am a part of that great cloud of witnesses, I'll be able to say thank you for your testimony of faith. Your faith encouraged me along the way.

An issue for any couple that is as inseparable as we are is the thought of standing alone before the Lord at the judgment seat of Christ. I will not stand before the Lord with Tom by my side. It is my responsibility to develop my own relationship with Christ. I do have a responsibility to be under my husband's headship. That position does not negate my responsibility before the Lord myself. There must be a delicate balance there.

Tom's job, as a pastor, is to exegete faithfully and teach the Word of God and shepherd the people of our church. I do not have a seminary degree, but I longed to be able to communicate with Tom in the area of his expertise. So, after almost thirty years, I became involved in inductive Bible studies. As Tom's helpmeet, I thoroughly enjoy an engaging discussion of the Scriptures. The added benefit came in that I began to long to spend more and more time in God's Word, not just for discussion with Tom but because I love God so for what he's done for me. By putting myself under Tom's headship and desiring to be a helpmeet for him, the Lord has given me what I needed, and that is a vibrant relationship with him.

Matthew 25:23 contains the words I long to hear when I stand before the Lord. If I faithfully trust the Lord for my strength, remember this life is but a short pilgrimage, realize my weeping will be rejoicing, and look daily to the Scriptures to remind me to go from strength to strength, I can hope to hear, "Well done, good and faithful servant." Wouldn't you love hearing those words, too?

CHAPTER FOURTEEN

In-laws

Dear Tony, David, Greg, and Becky—our in-laws,

To be perfectly honest, neither of us is fond of that in-law title. From the moment of your marriage to our children (and actually long before), we have thought of you as our own. We know that a marriage brings two families together. Each has a different history, different traditions, and ways of celebrating them, different approaches to problem solving, differing ideas about what is acceptable and what is not. The list is endless.

We want to be the kind of in-laws God intends for us to be. There are enough in-law jokes already, and we don't want to fit their stereotypes. We know that only the grace of God can make this possible, but we need your help as well. That's why I'm writing. This letter serves as an open, permanent invitation for you to share with us your views about how we can be the kind of in-laws who will bless you rather than create grief for you.

We know you might be hesitant to accept this invitation, especially at first. But you must. We believe that confrontations conducted in a *spirit of love and graciousness can be a positive experience. We trust that you feel the same.*

It's our desire to give you plenty of space. After all, cutting the apron strings doesn't mean you have to cut the heartstrings as well. So here we are. Let us know how we can be the kind of in-laws who only make the experiences in your marriage better. We look forward to hearing from you.

Love,

Dad

P.S. Now when it comes to rearing those grandkids, trust us! We know just how to spoil them.

Know the definition of *mixed emotions*? It's watching your mother-in-law drive over a cliff in your new automobile.

The penalty for polygamy? Having more than one mother-in-law.

Who said, "I don't know what I think about that; in fact, I haven't even heard what I've had to say about it yet"? Your father-in-law.

How many in-law jokes are there? One. All the rest are true.

The list is endless, isn't it? There's just something about in-laws that invites barbed, tongue-in-cheek humor. Unfortunately, most of the humor at the expense of in-laws is rooted in someone's sad, personal experience. It goes both ways. You do know that, considering the creep your daughter married, those beautiful grandchildren are proof that your own gene pool is incredibly healthy.

Meet Jethro, the model in-law. The daughter of this Midianite priest is none other than Zipporah, wife of Moses. Their sons, and his grandsons, are named Gershom and Eliezer. Now don't let these rather remarkable names ruin this for you! Jethro, in fact, is sometimes called Reuel, and perhaps at other times, Hobab.

A huge family problem erupts in a motel room on the trip from Midian back to Egypt where Moses is to confront Pharaoh and deliver Israel. (It always happens when you're moving to a new assignment and you have to sleep in the same room with the kids!) Moses insists that Gershom and Eliezer be circumcised. Zipporah complies under protest. There's a scene. Later that night, just when folks in the adjacent rooms are finally getting back to sleep, she packs up, grabs the kids, and heads back home, leaving Moses to pay the bill.

Undaunted and under orders, Moses continues on with his assistant, Aaron. They have a difficult but successful trip. Egypt is in shambles, the Egyptian army is decimated and drowned, the morticians are cleaning up, and Israel is delivered. Now they are on their way back to Canaan, defeating the enemies of God along the way.

One day, after a particularly grueling battle with the Amalekites, Moses looks up to see his father-in-law, Jethro, standing before him. Beside him are Zipporah, Gershom, and Eliezer. Moses' heart probably sank at that moment. It's one thing to handle the Amalekites and more than a million complaining Jews. It's another thing to face your father-in-law with your estranged wife peeking over his shoulder and your two sons who are still in counseling because of that night back in the motel, scowling at you from behind her skirt.

It's what happens next that makes Jethro the hero in this story. Notice the remarkable manner in which he handles the situation, leaving such a positive impression that Moses actually encourages Jethro to work side by side with him.

UNDERSTANDING THE RELATIONSHIP

When Jethro returned to Moses, bringing Moses' wife and children with him, it was not to upbraid him or to plead the cause of his daughter. Jethro understood that, once married, Zipporah and Moses belonged together. One can only imagine what transpired when she came in, weary and exhausted from what appeared to be nothing short of a harrowing experience. The average parent would have taken up her offense, welcomed her back home to stay, and sent a note of divorcement to her husband.

But not Jethro. He said, "Zipporah, you and your children belong with your husband. The misunderstanding can be resolved. Let's get packed, and I'll help you get back home where you belong. There you and Moses can work out your difficulties" (Exod. 18:1–6).

We're not encouraging a return to an abusive situation. The issue between Moses and Zipporah was actually a matter of his obedience to God. The point here is that Jethro, and all good in-laws, make clear that when people get married they start a whole new family. Issues will arise, but married couples need to work them out without parents taking upon themselves an offense for their child.

Many marriage conflicts are never resolved because of the tendency of in-laws to take sides, especially their own child's. I can recall a specific incident in which a young wife made an appointment to visit with me about her husband's seeming insensitivity. When she arrived at the office, she asked if her parents could come in with her. We had scarcely been seated when her father blurted out, "Preacher, I hope you can talk some sense into her husband. Nobody's going to treat my daughter like this and get by with it." Her parents, not really approving of the marriage in the first place, were only too eager to get her back home, in her old bedroom, where they could try again to raise her correctly.

It is the parents' responsibility to do all they can while their children are under their authority to ensure they marry God's choice for their mate. Once the marriage takes place, however, it is absolutely necessary for them to work through any relational problems without parental interference. If they do seek counsel from godly parents, it should be sought together. Yet parents should be cautious and discreet. Unsought advice simply creates more problems.

EXPRESSING GENUINE INTEREST

Jethro also expressed a loving and genuine interest in Moses' welfare and the work he was doing. They talked together about the mighty work of God among the Israelites. Jethro even went to work with Moses so he could understand more of the load his son-in-law was carrying. He became acquainted with Moses' associates. He asked serious and probing questions about the manner in which his work was conducted. The bottom line was this: Moses' father-in-law had a genuine interest in him, his work, and his family (Exod. 18:7–16).

Many in-laws are only vaguely acquainted with their child's mate, their interests, concerns, or the work they do. They ask few questions and do little to inform themselves. They simply don't care, and their lack of interest is communicated in many ways. As a result, they have little to discuss when together and only a vague notion of their children's concerns when they are apart.

Interest in another person is shown primarily through the art of listening. That is how we get to know God, for instance. "Be still, and know that I am God" (Ps. 46:10), He says. In other words, "Listen!" Listening is the way you show that you value your spouse, your children, or anyone for that matter. Generally older people cannot stand the thought of not giving advice. Yet good in-laws listen first.

Listen to Jethro's questions: "What are you doing? Why do you do this by yourself? Why do you sit as the people stand from morning until evening?" Jethro asked these questions after he observed Moses in his work of judging the people. If he had an idea to share, you didn't hear it just yet. His primary concern was in getting a good understanding of Moses' work. This was evidence of his genuine interest, and people listen to someone who really cares about them.

LEAVING ISSUES WITH GOD

Have you ever noticed that when some people get on an issue, they just hammer and hammer until they beat their subject into submission or generate wholesale rebellion? Notice how Jethro, the model in-law, handles the situation. In effect, he cautiously shares an idea (Exod. 18:17–26) but insists that Moses make sure God is commanding him regarding the matter. His advice made so much sense that Moses saw God in it, embraced it, and used it as Israel's new method of government.

Can you imagine what would have happened if Jethro had said, "Moses, this is stupid. Any idiot can see that you can't continue this. Where did you get such a harebrained idea in the first place? (A long sigh here.) Sit down, and I'll straighten out this mess for you." Jethro was willing to quietly offer counsel and leave the matter with God.

Some in-laws are bent on proving that they are better than either their child or the person their child married. They do not realize that, inadvertently, they are sending the signal that their child has made a poor choice in a mate and the only way they can survive is if the in-law pitches in and takes up the slack. It is as if they are in a contest for their child's affection and their son's or daughter-in-law's approval. At the end of each visit, they feel as if they have either won or lost, depending on how willing the young family has been to submit to their reasoning and do things their way.

One young couple said, "We love our parents. So why is it so difficult to get excited about their visits to our house? It seems that when they are there, we are constantly being told how little we know. And when they leave, we feel exhausted." There's a couple whose in-laws are unwilling to show an interest, give counsel if it is sought, and leave the issue with God. They are still trying to raise their children.

LEAVING WHEN IT'S TIME TO GO

There is an interesting conclusion to Jethro's visit with Moses. First, think about the incredible thing that has taken place. By all reason we would have thought that Jethro would have popped into camp, given him a piece of his mind (and Zipporah's), jumped on his camel, and ridden into the sunset never to be seen again. Instead, Zipporah and the boys are safely back with her husband and their father. Moses has a lifelong friend in his father-in-law. Jethro, in fact, has resolved one of the hairiest leadership problems Moses would ever encounter. Now, apparently at Jethro's own request, Moses "lets" him return to his own land (Exod. 18:27).

Jethro didn't overstay his welcome. When it was time to go home, he went home. When his work was finished, he left. As a matter of fact, Jethro probably never did wear out his welcome. Over the years his children and grandchildren probably longed for and eagerly anticipated every visit. Family relationships were so healthy that Moses later begged his father-in-law (or his brother-in-law, the meaning is uncertain) to be a scout for Israel on their journey. There was obviously a great deal of harmony between them. This doesn't happen if you have a tendency to "hang around past bedtime."

Some parents-in-law approach their children with the assumption that it is their responsibility to provide for them, beginning now. Oblivious to any schedule but their own, they come by, call, and insist on getting together to such an extent that their children are happier to see them go than come. We are reminded by the writer of Proverbs that there is value in "withdrawing our foot early" lest, in the end, "they grow weary and hate us" (Prov. 25:17). It is important to stay in touch. However, it is equally important to give folks their space and leave when it's time to go.

HOW SHOULD YOU RESPOND?

This may sound a little self-serving since we are in-laws. However, you cannot read this account of the homecoming without admitting that Moses did a few things right himself. Since this chapter is about in-laws, we feel it necessary to note that there is a proper response on behalf of children-in-law as well. Without dwelling on each issue, note that Moses set a standard for the manner in which a son-in-law (or daughter-in-law, for that matter) should respond to a mother-in-law or father-in-law:

1. You are to love them (Exod. 18:7).
2. You are to listen to them (Exod. 18:24).
3. You are to learn from them (Exod. 18:24).
4. You are to let them live the life God has ordered for them (Exod. 18:27).

That last quality is so important, especially in an era when people are experiencing longer and more active lives. God has a plan for all of us until the day He calls us home. Sometimes well-meaning children build a plan for their parents, ordered more around convenience than a clear sense of what God is about.

In the end it is a two-way street. There is no reason in-laws cannot get along with and mutually benefit one another throughout their lives. That, we are convinced, is the way God intended it. Together we can put an end to those in-law jokes.

CHAPTER FIFTEEN

A Legacy of Faith

Dear Kids,

We enjoyed the family reunion at the mountain lodge. What a wonderful time together! On the drive home we talked about our favorite moments and agreed that it was those late-night discussions after the kids were asleep. Just as when you were growing up, it seems those are the best times for opening up our hearts to one another.

The discussion regarding the legacy we each hope to leave was especially encouraging to us, and not just because it had little to do with material resources! I think we all agree that the greatest inheritance is a legacy of faith. Your interpretation of Proverbs 13:22 is exactly right. The inheritance left by a "good man" to his grandchildren is certainly more than mere money! It is the legacy of his "goodness." In fact we are reminded that "a good name is to be chosen over great riches" (Prov. 22:1).

How can we ensure that each of us passes along a legacy of faith? That question kept surfacing in our discussion. It's one to which we have given considerable thought ever since. One thing we have observed: it takes a long time to build such a legacy but little time to destroy it!

You can be assured that we're going to spend more time thinking through this issue. Let's pray for one another that each of us will be most remembered for passing along a legacy of faith.

Love,

Dad and Mom

It was one of those tense moments that ultimately became a turning point in the life of a young building contractor. If he backed away from his request, he would lose any of the profit originally anticipated. What's more, it would cost him an additional amount sufficient to exhaust his resources and perhaps bankrupt his company. So now he had come to admit his mistake in drawing up the bid and ask for more money.

"Absolutely not!" was the terse reply as the signed contract was waved in his face. "This is your bid and your signature. We chose you over several others because of it. We trusted you to do your homework. You should have included a margin for cost increases. It's too late now to change. You gave us your word."

"That last statement settled the issue for me," the contractor recounted. "He was right! I did give him my word, and I had to keep it regardless of what it did to me or my company." Then he shared why keeping his word was so important.

"You see," he continued, "I inherited this business from my father. On more than one occasion I have seen him eat his profits and, in fact, go in the hole in order to keep his word. Dad would remind me that all we had to trade on was our integrity, and if we sacrificed that, we could not depend on the Lord to bless us. To him it was more than a matter of integrity; it was a matter of faith in God. He often told us that when he took Christ as his Savior he also made Him the CEO of his company. He never wanted to do anything that would give his 'Boss' a bad reputation." This man's father had left him a legacy of faith, something worth far more than great riches.

THE GREATEST GIFT YOU CAN GIVE YOUR FAMILY

"I had a grandmother who was a believer," a man once told me as he sat across from me in my office, "and she was my favorite. I always wanted what she had. Do you think it's possible?" As we shared for a few more minutes, he became the beneficiary of his grandmother's legacy of faith.

You can give your family members no greater gift than a legacy of faith. When King Solomon stated that "a good man leaves an inheritance to his children's children" (Prov. 13:22 NASB), he was most likely referring to earthly wealth. That is good advice as far as it goes. It is unfortunate that in spite of leaving a sizable fortune for his grandchildren, Solomon was not, in the end, remembered for his faith. Sadly, the compromises of his later years resulted in a divided family and a divided kingdom. Better for us all that he had focused on leaving a legacy of faith!

In his second letter to Timothy, the apostle Paul reminds his young protégé that the "unfeigned faith" which Timothy possessed resided first in his grandmother, Lois, and his mother, Eunice (2 Tim. 1:5). They had passed on to him a legacy of faith. It's impossible to give away something you don't originally possess. As personal as salvation is, there is a sense in which we receive it as a gift passed along from God to us by others. Paul was reminding Timothy of his spiritual roots.

One winter, while away from home on our annual time together, Jeannie and I had a serious talk about what we most desired to leave our children. We both decided that the most important treasure we could pass along would be a legacy of faith. In fact, these words are recorded in my journal: "My greatest desire is that I would be a living illustration of God's faithfulness to those who are simply willing to take Him at His Word."

Before we returned home, we received word that our house had burned to the ground. We thought it interesting (in light of our discussion) that not one thing was lost in the fire that we felt was crucial for our children to inherit. We saw, in fact, that the manner in which we responded had the potential for even increasing the inheritance we wanted them to receive, a legacy of faith.

A POINT OF BEGINNING

Every legacy of faith has its point of beginning. I am blessed to be in a family which has in it several generations of preachers. At the most recent count, there are fifteen preachers spread across four generations. But as best we can tell, our family's legacy of faith stretches back at least two more generations. It was then that a young mother on a train headed back East fell seriously ill. It soon became evident she would die. Calling her unbelieving husband to kneel beside the bench where she lay dying, she made him promise to give not only himself but their new child to God. The next Sunday in a small country church, a rough, angular man stood to testify. Holding his small child in the air, he said, "Brethren, I have given my life to God and have come today to be baptized." My father is named after that man whose wife's plea marks the beginning point for our family's legacy of faith.

"There was a beginning point for your faith," Paul reminded Timothy. "It dwelt first in your grandmother." With those words we are reminded that every legacy of faith has its point of beginning. Occasionally when telling our family's story, I am confronted by someone who laments, "But I didn't receive a wonderful heritage of faith."

That simply means you have the privilege of being the first in line, the beginning point, for generations to come. What an awesome privilege! Have you thanked God for the honor? Are you passing along the faith God has given you? Our family is thankful for that young mother who in her dying moment passed along a legacy of faith.

Family reunions are a great time for recounting your family's own legacy of faith. It is important that each member of your family possess some sense of the spiritual heritage that is to be passed on from generation to generation.

IT'S UNDER YOUR WATCH!

Recently we witnessed the removal of a high-ranking naval officer because of a tragic and costly incident. Although the mistake in judgment was not actually made by this man, he was the commanding officer, and it happened under his watch. How is your family's legacy of faith faring under your watch? Is it developing or disappearing?

Timothy's grandmother made certain that the torch of her faith was passed to her daughter who then passed it to her own son. That is not always the case. On more than one occasion I have talked with parents whose own children "came to church faithfully" but have now "strayed from the faith." Admittedly, we cannot discount the power of personal choice. After all, remember the prodigal son! Neither can we pass the buck when it comes to nurturing a growing sense of spiritual heritage. Churches don't raise children; parents do! Under your care the legacy of faith grows or withers.

I see it often as a pastor. The extended family gathers for the celebration of a fiftieth wedding anniversary. Many of them stay for church the next morning, sometimes occupying several rows in the auditorium. As I look across those rows, I see the proud celebrants and rejoice in both their faith and their faithfulness. But then I notice that each successive generation seems to have become more distant from both Christ and His church. What is a thrilling service for the great-grandparents is only endured by others who feel (and sometimes act) strangely out of place.

It's not always that way! On other occasions the entire family seems at home. They love the privilege of worship and, in fact, stay around long after the service to fellowship with friends or to meet the pastor. With pride the elderly couple introduce each family member and tell where they live and what church they attend.

A legacy of faith is not wished into existence. It takes prayer, personal interest, and participation. I sometimes get the impression that a few folks think they can just wake up in the morning, fall out of bed, and pass along a legacy of faith. It requires much more! It requires what a friend calls, "Finishing well." A legacy of faith is like a flame. It requires tending.

INCREDIBLE IMPACT!

Timothy was the recipient of at least two letters penned by the apostle Paul. Those two letters, inspired by the Holy Spirit, are some of the most significant letters in the New Testament. While we know little of Lois or Eunice, we know a great deal about Timothy. You cannot help but wonder if his mother and grandmother ever imagined that, one day, Paul would place his ministerial mantle upon Timothy. That's the incredible impact inherent in a legacy of faith.

Years ago, when Jeannie and I were just engaged, I took her to visit my grandparents on my father's side of the family. My grandfather took her hand in his, held it to his lips, and kissed it! Then, with a twinkle in his eye, he said, "That's an old Elliff custom, and I'm the old Elliff who started it!" That's not all he and my grandmother started.

My grandfather was a preacher who in his early days was a hard-hitting, Bible-thumping, barnstorming, brush arbor, exhorter of the brethren. Preaching up and down the border between Arkansas and Oklahoma, he often stirred such controversy that possees would be called out to protect him. On one occasion the music for a revival was provided through instruments belonging to the Anti-Horse Thief Band. My grandmother, on the other hand, while a quiet and gracious lady, was the greatest soul-winner I ever knew, leading dozens to the Lord the very year of her death.

When they were in their eighties, I began pastoring a small country church in a town near where they lived. Generally, as I made my way back to college on Sunday evenings, I would stop by their home with a carload of friends. My grandparents would fix a late-night breakfast and talk about the Lord. It is impossible to relate just how formative those discussions were for my friends and me. We always left with prayer, encouragement, and full stomachs. My grandparents were determined that their latest days would be their greatest days, and they were!

My youngest brother, Bill, is the gifted pastor of the dynamic Summit Church in Little Rock, Arkansas. He is also our family's poet laureate. This poem of his, read at a family reunion as a charge to our children, reveals the incredible impact of a legacy of faith:

God has done a wondrous work down through the family line, as
    one by one,
He's called men out to walk with Christ through time.

And now the Lord has called your name, this heritage to share,
For He has passed this torch to you and on to those you rear.
Our God desires to multiply His work yet more and more,
Each generation gaining from the one that's gone before,
'Til growing tides of godliness like waves upon the shore,
Build tidal waves of praise to Him, both now and evermore.
And so your family from above watches from the heavenly
    stands.
The gathered wealth of all God's done is placed within your
    hands,
To run the race with faithfulness, with holiness, with truth,
'Til God's work is perfected, and our family's task is through.

The bottom line is this: Whatever you do, leave a legacy of faith and faithfulness.